Ste

May you or others
you know never
have to?

BEAT THE BOSS

Win in the Workplace

Spencer Cohn

ISBN: 978-0-692-38192-2

Disclaimer:

The information provided in this book is designed to provide helpful information on the subjects discussed. The accuracy and completeness of information provided herein and opinions stated herein are not guaranteed or warranted to produce any particular results, and the advice and strategies contained herein may not be suitable for everyone. The author and publisher shall not be liable for any loss or damage incurred as a consequence of any errors or omissions involving or related to the use or application, directly or indirectly, of any advice or information presented in this book resulting from negligence, gross negligence, and/or any other cause whatsoever on the part of the author and/or publisher. Although this book is designed to provide accurate information, it is sold and distributed with the understanding that the author and publisher are not engaged in rendering legal, or other professional services. If any such advice or expert assistance is required, the services of a competent professional should be sought. Information in this book relates to subjects that are changing regularly. References are provided for informational purposes only and do not constitute endorsement of any websites or other sources. Readers should be aware that the websites listed in this book may change. Further, users of any such websites are urged to carefully review the terms of use and privacy policies of such sites, as applicable.

Acknowledgement

To my Mom and Dad who have always been there for me, and to my beautiful wife and best friend who has guided and loved me through the years.

Forward

I was first introduced to Mr. Cohn while at Fox News working on a segment about workplace issues.

My name is Lisa Carton, and as an award-winning journalist, I've worked in television and radio news as a reporter for over a decade. I began my career in the San Francisco Bay area covering local and national stories for KTVU, KRON, KGO Radio, and CNET. From San Francisco, I joined FOX News radio in New York as a national correspondent. I spent several years crisscrossing the country covering the horror that was Hurricane Katrina, on the trail of missing teen Natalie Holloway, uncovering The Balco Steroid scandal, "live" field coverage of two Super Bowls, watching the tragedy of Virginia Tech unfold, and seeing the return of Sgt. Bowe Bergdahl to the U.S., just to name a few.

To accomplish my job duties it was not unusual to rely on co-workers to "get the job done". However on other occasions, I did utter the familiar phrase, "I was thrown ꓱer the bus." At certain periods of my tenure, I ꓱnced poor management, and those who I would characterize as not exactly qualified in their positions. Although I may be describing my experience at Fox News as tedious and riddled with problems- it was not. I was grateful to grow as a professional, gaining a level of experience that was unmatched and proud to work with many talented colleagues.

However, there were incidents at work which I felt fell under the guise of unfair treatment at the workplace...it wasn't just a matter of developing "thick skin." The incidents which occurred were not enough for me to walk into a lawyer's office and pay a fee for advice, but enough for me to ask someone for help.

For instance, I remember an incident when my superiors assigned me a story which involved immediately jumping on a plane. I reminded them of my faulty equipment that I had alerted them to before, and the response was, "work it out" or "take it to engineering." As a result, this caused delays in getting to my destination and timely coverage of a story. Another incident involved a co-worker becoming extremely jealous and angry that I received a high profile assignment over her, and as a result sprouted lies about me for her gain. I ignored this petty newsroom nonsense, but at some point it began to interfere with my work. I finally decided to consult with my immediate supervisor who did nothing, and then ultimately turned to Human Resources, where I was made to feel defensive, and quickly became aware they were not there to assist me...they were there to protect the employer.

I consulted Spencer Cohn and his expertise was invaluable. He assisted with my workplace issues, and helped me to resolve them by offering me guidance to responses and behavior, which ultimately remedied my obstacles at work. This allowed me to do my job and do it well.

When Mr. Cohn approached me about writing the forward to his book, knowing what he does for workplace rights and issues, I accepted without hesitation. This book is far more valuable than any employee handbook you will ever receive. It's filled with insightful and helpful information you can't get anywhere else. The funny and shocking anecdotes is an easy read that arms you with the knowledge that may prevent some of the unfortunate incidents that occur in the workplace, from happening to you. You can pick this book up at any chapter, and you will glean some great information. Mr. Cohn pulls back the curtain of what really happens between the hours of 9 and 5.

Introduction

When I first was introduced to the working world, I must have been 4 or 5 years old, watching my father dress in the morning for work. He had a very meticulous manner as he shaved, and the clothes he selected were always pressed and stylishly coordinated. He either wore a suit or a sport jacket and tie and regularly shined his own shoes. He was very proud he wasn't working for anyone - he was the boss. I remember asking him, "Where you going?" My father responded, "Work. Someday you'll be old enough to do the same…it won't be long. I started working when I was 10 years old, and pretty soon young man, you'll understand what going to work is all about."

To the best of my memory, my first job was raking leaves and cutting grass, and I wasn't fond of either. I should say I liked using the lawn mower because I thought the machine was pretty cool, but that feeling passed very quickly. Raking leaves back then manually done, taking hours to do, and longer when it was windy. Adding to the problem, I was allergic to grass, so that didn't make things any easier. Aside from our lawn, I got the unenviable job of cutting my neighbor's huge yard. The pay was fine, but I had to contend with these pesky Purple Martins, which if you're not familiar, are these small, shiny, dark purple birds that would dart in and out around me while I was cutting the grass. I know they were trying to catch the insects that were stirred up by the lawnmower, but they made it difficult for a 13 year-old and also scared the life out of me! I use to complain to my neighbor, but he just chuckled as it fell on deaf ears. I performed my duties in full armor wearing my Philadelphia Eagles football helmet with sunglasses, while wielding a wiffle bat for protection as I drove the lawnmower. I suppose to the onlooker it must have been hysterical, but to me it was work...my first paying job, and I took it very seriously.

I moved through various jobs through the years including working for my father in his stores selling jewelry and appliances, a mover for a national transit company, and as a summer job, I worked for the Southern New Jersey Mosquito Commission counting bugs in the various traps, so each county knew where and when to spray. In my later years after law school, I worked as a bailiff for the Miami courthouse, and then went on to clerking in law firms, before eventually beginning my own practice.

However, I do recall one employer specifically- a father and son law firm. The father was a pretty crafty and intelligent man, but the son was a wannabe big shot. Of course I got stuck working for the son. It was a miserable experience. He talked endlessly about nothing, incessantly smoking cigars when his father wasn't around. His breath was intolerable and he certainly wasn't the sharpest tool in the shed. But I hung in there because the salary was great. But one day, after tolerating one more day of mindless chatter and cigar smoke, I had enough. I impulsively left a note on the son's office chair, "Too nice a day to be inside" and left my key. I was outta there.

The point of detailing my job history is that I worked as an employee for many years, and I get it. I understand what the worker faces besides just performing his or her duties. In my current practice, I'm exposed to employee issues each day through numerous unemployment hearings, and I'm an expert in workplace law and its issues. I understand more than most, the challenges employees face day after day, month after month, and year after year.

To be fair, there are thousands of honest employers that provide good working environments, and I commend them for their fair standards. However, *my* crusade is to help level the playing field for the average worker. This book is a compilation of short stories that offers the employee good practical information for navigating the workplace and I'm happy to share my expertise with you.

Contents

The Stories

"Don't Come Back"

Allison works as a seamstress for a multimillion-dollar dress manufacturer, at the rate of $12 per hour. She's one of twenty-five seamstresses in her department. And even though Allison has been a reliable worker for six years, her boss Joan treats her as disposable.

Allison makes high-end dresses to precise specifications, and always under very tight deadlines. It's typical for Joan to give Allison the material and design for a dress and tell her to complete it in twenty hours.

The atmosphere in Allison's workplace is continually tense. Part of this is due to the short deadlines, coupled with Joan's demands for perfection. But it's also because of Joan's personal style.

To be blunt, Joan has a gutter mouth. And on top of the profanity, Joan is verbally abusive.

One day Joan walks over to Allison and literally drops material and specs into her lap. "Stop what you're doing immediately," says Joan, "and work on this new dress. It must be completed in eighteen hours."

Allison timidly raises her eyes and says, "Okay. But just so you know, I have only about fifteen minutes to go on this dress I'm finishing up."

Joan harshly responds, "Do as I say. Now!" Allison nods assent.

A few hours later, Joan comes over to check on Allison's progress. Joan sees Allison is having trouble with the spool. Joan then looks at the dress and notices the sleeves seem shorter than what's required by the specs. Without even asking what Allison has in mind, Joan lashes out with a barrage of obscenities in front of Allison's co-workers, saying such things as "Allison! You are a dumbass!! I'm paying you way too much. You couldn't sew a patch on a pair of jeans!"

Allison turns red. In a soft voice, she replies, "I'm following the specifications you gave me."

Joan screams, "No you're not! You're incompetent!!"

With all the dignity she can muster, Allison gets up from her chair, picks up her purse and starts walking to the door.

"Where do you think you're going!?!" yells Joan.

"I'm going home," Allison replies. "I've told you in the past that I don't appreciate you speaking to me this way, yet you continue to insult me."

Joan glares at her. "If you leave now, don't come back."

Allison walks out the door and goes home.

Has Allison quit her job?

Answer to *"Don't Come Back:"*

Allison didn't quit.

Allison never said she was leaving forever. She didn't even take her personal belongings with her, which she would have done if she had no intention of returning. She was merely removing herself at that moment from an intolerable situation.

However, Joan *fired* Allison.

Joan's abusive behavior, coupled with her ultimatum—"If you leave now, don't come back"—can be considered what the law calls a *constructive discharge* or *constructive termination*.

It would be more straightforward if Joan had said, "If you leave now, you're fired." But the real world often isn't that tidy, and labor law recognizes this.

That said, Allison should return the next day at her scheduled shift. If Joan tells her that she no longer works for her, then Allison can immediately file for unemployment benefits.

If Joan adds, "Your leaving yesterday meant you quit, so don't expect severance or unemployment payments," Allison can calmly respond that she didn't quit, and that she'll be writing up everything that happened in detail to make it clear Joan fired her. Allison's notes will be useful if she has to go to court…or, for that matter, report Joan to the corporation's HR department.

Guarding Her Children's Safety

Sharla is a night security guard. When Sharla filled out her job application, she checked off the "Can be flexible with hours" box because she desperately needed to be hired. In reality, though, she can work only nights because she's a single mom with two young children. Sharla's mother works during the day and then comes over at night to look after the kids.

For five years, this arrangement works fine. Then Sharla is injured and has to take a couple of months off. When she's ready to come back to work, her night shift position has been filled. A day shift is open, though, so Sharla's assigned to return to work Monday at 9:00 am.

A few days before she's scheduled to come back, Sharla calls her manager. "I'm really sorry," Sharla says, "but I can't start on Monday. I have two small children, and I'm having trouble finding someone to be with them. I need a night shift; or if that's not possible, two weeks to find appropriate childcare."

"I'm sorry too," says Sharla's manager, "but I need someone to fill the day shift on Monday, and you're the only one available. If you don't come in, I'll have to fire you and replace you with someone who wants the job."

"Okay," says Sharla. "I'll be there."

On Monday, Sharla reports at 9:00 am as promised. However, she goes straight to her manager to complain. "You have to put me back on nights," she says. "I found a neighbor to stay with my kids today, but he won't be able to do it again tomorrow."

"I understand," her manager replies, "but I just don't have any other shifts open right now."

"Then give me two weeks to find another solution. I can't come back here tomorrow. It would mean leaving my kids by themselves in the apartment, and that's just too dangerous."

"I appreciate your situation, but you need to appreciate mine. If you don't come in tomorrow, I'll have to assume you've abandoned your job and will start looking for a replacement."

Sharla looks her manager in the eye and says, "I'm not abandoning my job. I'm just taking care of my children. I won't be in the rest of this week."

The next day, true to her word, Sharla doesn't come to work. She doesn't come in for the rest of the week either.

The following Monday Sharla receives a final paycheck in the mail...along with a termination letter stating that she abandoned her job by refusing an assignment.

Sharla sighs, and applies for unemployment benefits.

Will she receive them?

Answer to *Guarding Her Children's Safety:*

Sharla will probably receive her benefits.

Sharla stated on her job application that she could be flexible with her hours, which weighs against her not taking the day shift.

However, Sharla's request for two weeks to secure childcare is a fair one. At an unemployment benefits hearing, a judge is likely to rule Sharla's employer was being unreasonable in not giving her the chance to meet the challenges to her kids' safety created by the change to her schedule.

The employer could counter that Sharla's absence during those two weeks would have adversely affected it, because other employees would've had to work extra hard and/or the business would've been forced to slow down. Both of these reasons are often brought up at hearings; but unless the employer can clearly substantiate them, judges usually disregard them.

"I Don't Accept"

Recently unemployed and short on cash, Bruce is delighted when he spots an ad for a telemarketing position that promises forty hours of work a week. It involves making cold calls to potential customers, and being paid for each call that's completed—meaning the caller either gets through the entire script or makes a sale on the spot. Bruce likes that he gets paid whether the customer buys right away or not.

Bruce gets an interview, and it's the smoothest one he's ever had—within fifteen minutes, he's hired. The interviewer, named Vinny, gives Bruce the script he must follow for the sales call, and also a personal ID code. Vinny explains, "You've gotta enter this code into one of our special telemarketing phones before any call. The conversation will then be automatically recorded, enabling your manager to check on how many calls you completed under that code. That'll determine how much you're paid at the end of each week." Bruce happily agrees.

The next day, Bruce shows up for work. To his surprise, he's placed in a room with over fifty other telemarketers…and just twenty-five phones. Every phone is being actively used. The other telemarketers are just sitting around chatting casually with each other. Bruce asks a woman, "Why are you all just sitting here?" She replies, "We're waiting for one of the phones to open up," and then returns to her conversation. Bruce pinches himself to make sure he's not in a dream.

Bruce gently taps the woman on the shoulder. "I'm sorry to bother you, but I don't understand. What do you mean you're waiting for the phones?" The woman chuckles and says, "A call only 'counts' if it's made on a company phone, and there are only twenty-five of those. So we have to wait until someone is ready to stop calling and give up the phone to someone else. You can take a number over there"—she points to a machine that dispenses numbers on slips of paper—"and then get a phone when your number is called."

"How long is that going to take?" Bruce asks. "Your guess is as good as mine," she answers. "Yesterday I waited four hours until I was able to get on."

Bruce is not happy. He looks out the window and spots Vinny in the parking lot about to get into a car. Bruce dashes out and says, "Excuse me, Vinny, but there's a problem." Vinny looks at Bruce, barely remembering who he is, and replies, "Yeah, buddy, what's up?"

Bruce says, "I was just put in a room with way more telemarketers than phones." Vinny nods casually. "Yeah, don't worry about it. People leave all the time because they get bored or hungry or need to go to the bathroom or whatever, and then you can jump in."

Bruce is stunned. "I don't understand. The ad promised I'd be working 40 hours a week. But if the phones aren't available, I can't make the calls—which means I can't make my hours." Vinny starts up his car, rolls down the window and says, "Just work it out with the other telemarketers." Vinny makes a thumbs-up sign, and then drives off.

Bruce is disgusted. He looks for the company's HR office, walks into it, and tells the unnaturally cheery woman there, "This job isn't what I expected. I can't continue here."

"I'm sorry it didn't work out," she chirps. "Please just turn in a letter of resignation for our records before you leave."

Should Bruce write the letter?

Answer to *"I Don't Accept:"*

No. Bruce can't resign from a job that he never accepted.

The company's description of the job was grossly misleading. Bruce's hours and earnings depended on his making calls on a company phone, and it was never explained that he wouldn't be assigned a phone he could use at all times. Also, Bruce was promised 40 hours of work, but that's impossible to achieve under the current set-up. Bruce never even began performing the services he was hired for because he wasn't provided the necessary equipment to do so.

Since the employment relationship was never formed, Bruce can't be said to have quit.

The company wants Bruce's resignation on record so it's not liable for Bruce's unemployment benefits. However, the company is equally not liable if Bruce refuses the job, so it's fine either way.

On the other hand, how Bruce responds to HR's request will make a huge difference to *him*. If he says, "I don't accept this job, so can't quit" and leaves, he's fine.

But if Bruce does as asked and officially resigns, his unemployment payments will stop; and he won't be able to file for them again for 12 months. Since Bruce is already barely hanging on financially, that means Bruce wouldn't only be out a job; he'd soon be out on the street for inability to pay rent.

The lesson here is to never do something just because HR asks you to. Always seriously consider the potential consequences.

The Aspiring Translator

Jose works in a fast food restaurant in Los Angeles as a cook. He's fluent in Spanish, and that comes in handy because the cashier often needs assistance translating a Hispanic customer's order. Jose is glad to help out because it provides a chance to take a break from the hot kitchen and shoot the breeze with the cashier.

Unfortunately, the store's assistant manager Rod doesn't approve of how much time Jose spends at the front of the store. Rod frequently reminds Jose, "*Translator* isn't part of your job description. Focus on the cooking."

One day Rod sees Jose at the register chatting with a drop-dead gorgeous brunette. It seems clear to Rod that Jose is doing nothing but flirting with the customer.

Rod rushes over to Jose and says, "What do you think you're doing?"

"I'm translating!" Jose replies.

"Sure you are," Rod says. "I've told you a thousand times, you're a cook and you have no business up here at the register."

"But I—" Jose begins.

"No! No more excuses," Rod states bluntly. "I'll take over the kitchen for the rest of your shift. Just leave—before I lose my temper."

Jose starts to open his mouth…but then looks into Rod's eyes and thinks better of it. Jose angrily throws down his apron and exits the store.

The next day, Jose stays home and files for unemployment.

Will Jose receive his benefits?

Answer to *The Aspiring Translator:*

Jose blew it.

An employee is considered to be fired if the words and actions of the employer lead a reasonable person to believe that termination has occurred. Rod told Jose to leave, but he didn't say anything permanent such as "Leave forever" or "I never want to see you again." It is possible Rod was so angry at that moment that he simply didn't want to deal with Jose until after calming down.

Jose was wrong to not come into work the next day and make every effort to clarify his employment status. He assumed he was fired; but by not showing up at the restaurant and not calling in, he effectively quit. Jose messed up both his chance to keep his job and his opportunity to collect unemployment from the restaurant...because while he was a good translator, he was ultimately a poor communicator.

A Dispute Over Specs

Tom works for a prestigious architectural company and earns a salary in the high six figures. His boss Sandy is an older man who doesn't mince words. Tom believes that Sandy holds him in high regard and has plans to eventually invite him to be a partner in the firm.

Tom's spent three long, hard months designing a building for a major client. Just before the deadline, Tom submits the blueprint to Sandy, saying "Here you go. This one wasn't easy; too many arches and pillars to my liking. But it's what the client wants."

"Great," says Sandy. "The client actually flew into town a little early and will be coming over this afternoon, so your timing is perfect. I'll look it over now to prepare myself."

Tom smiles, and returns to his desk feeling good about himself. But less than 10 minutes later Sandy comes rushing at him, looking furious, and hurls the blueprints down at his feet with great force.

Tom is utterly startled. "What's going on?" he asks.

A red-faced Sandy grabs Tom's tie, uses it to yank Tom up from his seat, and screams, "Listen, you moron, don't ever submit crap like this to me again! This blueprint is *not* done to specs. I have to call one of our biggest clients and tell him we've had an emergency that'll delay the presentation, because he'll see this junk over my dead body!!"

Sandy then releases Tom's tie and storms out.

Tom doesn't know what hit him. He's sure he followed the specs that were given to him, and wonders if Sandy was examining either an older or newer version. But more importantly, Tom has never seen Sandy behave that way before…and it really shakes him up.

Sitting just 10 feet from Tom is his secretary Joanie, who witnessed the entire incident. Tom turns to her and says, "Did you see that? Sandy just assaulted me!" Joanie is silent and noncommittal, not sure where her loyalties should lie.

"I'm leaving," Tom declares. "If Sandy wants me, he can pick up the phone to discuss what happened. I'll wait for his call at home." Tom then walks out.

Thirty minutes later, a much calmer Sandy returns to Tom's office. "Joanie, do you know where Tom is?" he asks.

"He left," is Joanie's only response.

"That's fine. It saves me the trouble," says Sandy. "Have HR place an ad online for an architect as soon as possible."

Because Joanie failed to convey Tom's message, Sandy never calls Tom; and Tom never speaks again to Sandy.

Did Tom do the right thing? And was Tom fired, or did he quit?

Answer to *A Dispute Over Specs:*

Even though Tom was thrown off-balance by Sandy's shocking behavior, Tom's responses were inexcusably inept.

Tom was right to leave the office. However, he should've headed directly to his local police station to file an assault report. The police would then have followed up by taking Joanie's testimony. This would've provided an official record of the incident difficult for Sandy to dispute.

Also, right after speaking to the police, Tom should've sent an email, a fax, or a registered letter to his firm's HR department complaining about the assault. The document should've stated Tom's belief that Sandy fired him, and requested confirmation.

Because none of these things happened, if this case comes to trial a judge will have only Tom's word against Sandy's—plus Joanie's testimony. If Joanie accurately recalls Sandy's actions, and reports that after Tom left Sandy said, "That's fine. It saves me the trouble," then it'll be clear Tom was fired. But since Joanie is still getting paid by Sandy's firm, it's quite possible that over time she'll come to remember events the way Sandy wants her to.

The lesson here is to record any critical incident, and report it to the proper authorities through a trackable message system, as soon as possible. And when assault is involved, don't hesitate to involve the police.

"Get Your Stuff and Get Out"

Mindy doesn't know why, but her manager Renee has made her the scapegoat for anything that goes wrong at the office. If a file is lost or a report is late, regardless of who's officially in charge of it, Renee finds a way to point a finger at Mindy. And Renee follows this up with major screaming.

Mindy isn't confrontational, so she endures this crazed behavior for 10 months. Then one day Mindy's best friend visits at the end of the day and witnesses a particularly loud tirade from Renee. The friend is amazed that Mindy just takes it. "Are you kidding me?!" she says. "You have to quit!"

Mindy can't argue. The next day she walks into the office holding a sheet of paper. Without asking permission, Renee snatches it out of her hand and sarcastically snarls, "What's this?" Mindy responds, "It's my resignation letter. I'm giving two week's notice."

Mindy expects Renee to throw her biggest tantrum ever. Instead, Renee becomes very quiet. She goes into her office and stays there for the rest of the day, not speaking to anyone.

Over the next week, Mindy tells her co-workers that she'll be leaving. She keeps expecting a blow-up from Renee, but things remain surprisingly calm.

Five days before she's scheduled to leave, a co-worker asks for Mindy's personal email address so they can stay in touch. Mindy replies, "Call me at home for it tonight, I don't want Renee to know it. Did you see her today? I think she's drunk." Mindy then turns around—and finds Renee standing right behind her, steaming.

"Mindy!" Renee screeches. "You're done!! Give me your office key! Get your stuff and get out!!!" Mindy is so startled that at first she freezes. After a few moments, though, Mindy composes herself, gathers her belongings, and leaves without saying another word.

Did Mindy quit, or was she fired?

Answer to *"Get Your Stuff and Get Out:"*

Mindy was fired.

While Mindy's resignation happened first, Renee overrode it by choosing to discharge Mindy before the date she was scheduled to leave.

Because Renee's temper didn't allow her to wait the few extra days they'd agreed Mindy would stay on, Mindy is entitled to unemployment benefits. It should be noted that generally in most states, if the employee provides a definitive date of resignation and is fired before the date specified, the employee would be entitled to unemployment benefits up to said date and then thereafter the employee's separation would be treated as a quit.

Sick with Case of Bad Boss

Bill works as a salesman for an office supply company. Bill enjoyed his job under his previous manager; but his new boss Kristoff has turned a friendly environment into a high-pressured one, with weekly sales quotas and a great deal of shouting. For example, Kristoff tends to start off the day with, "This all you sell yesterday? Is this joke? Monkey sell more than this! I should replace you with monkey!!"

Bill develops migraine headaches, shortness of breath, and fatigue. When his doctor interviews Bill and runs tests, he determines the cause to be job-related stress. His doctor recommends quitting, but Bill is nervous about re-entering the market at his age.

After two years of Kristoff and ill health, Bill begins having trouble meeting his sales goals. When Kristoff screams at him about it, Bill counters that it's Kristoff's fault for turning him into a physical wreck.

"Ridiculous!" yells Kristoff. "You talk like woman. You should wear dress. Put on high heels and go sell supplies!!"

Bill goes on medication for high blood pressure. He informs Kristoff's boss about what's going on, and also the HR department. Nothing changes except for Kristoff getting angrier. "Company say somebody complain! It picnic here!! At age five I enlist in army to feed family! I kill 50 men by age seven! You sit on fat ends and talk on phone! Today you all stand like soldiers. Stand all day!!"

After another month goes by, Bill's heart starts pounding in his chest. His doctor expresses concern for Bill's life if he doesn't cut out the stress, and soon.

The next day, Kristoff screams at Bill, "Get numbers up, old man, or I kick you end so hard end it move to zipper! I knock you head so powerful it drop down to you high heels! I been much too kind. No more!!"

"That's it," says Bill. "I quit." Without another word, Bill picks up his things and walks out the door.

The next day Bill files for unemployment. His company challenges the claim, saying he left of his own free will, forcing Bill to go to court. Will he win?

Answer to *Sick with Case of Bad Boss:*

Bill won twice-over.

His doctor provided documentation showing that Bill had to leave his job for medical reasons. That was enough to ensure Bill's unemployment compensation.

Under normal circumstances the state would've covered the payments for a medical-related resignation.

Because his company pushed him to court, however, Bill had to explain how he became ill. The judge determined it was a hostile work environment that gave Bill no choice but to quit. The judge therefore ordered Bill's compensation be charged to his employer.

As a result, Bill not only won his benefits, but the satisfaction of knowing his company would be paying for them. The next day both his heart rate and blood pressure started heading down to healthy levels.

off the mark.com
by Mark Parisi
NO WHITE MEAT?!! YOU NINCOMPOOP! YOU'D BETTER THINK OF SOMETHING OR IT'S YOUR JOB!
BLEACH
offthemark.com
ATLANTIC FEATURE
© 1992 MARK PARISI
MARK PARISI

Paying for a Mistake

Leon supervises 10 forklifts in a large warehouse. His responsibilities are to keep the vehicles in great shape, manage their operators, and ensure all crates are delivered to the company's dock on schedule for pick-up and transport.

Leon is a stickler about maintenance, insisting his workers check oil levels at least twice a week. But despite this, one day an awful burning smell comes wafting through the air. Leon quickly realizes it's the result of a motor burning up.

Spotting the crippled forklift, Leon runs to its operator and shouts, "Jeff, what the hell's happening?!"

"I don't know," Jeff says. "The thing just died on me."

Smoke starts pouring out of the hood. Leon grabs a fire extinguisher and sprays it down. When the smoke clears, it's apparent the engine is burned out.

"For god sakes, Jeff!" Leon is furious. "Did you check the oil levels before taking it out?"

Jeff looks at the ground. "I thought I did."

Leon opens the oil cap and sees that it's dry. He also sees that the head gasket has blown, making the forklift useless.

A few moments later, the company's owner Bernie runs down—and lets loose on Leon. "Why are you jumping on Jeff?!" demands Bernie. "He don't know better! Damn it, Leon, it's your job to stay on top of these morons! That machine is ruined, and it's your fault!! Give me one reason I shouldn't fire you."

"Bernie, please," says Leon, "we're not even sure why it happened. Maybe the gauge was defective, or maybe there was a slow leak no one could've noticed."

"Excuses aren't going to get me a working forklift!!" screams Bernie. "Your job is to take care of my equipment by overseeing these idiots, but looks to me you've become one of them! Leon, there's the door unless you cough up $15,000 for a new forklift."

Leon gasps. "Are you serious?"

"As a heart attack," says Bernie. "If you don't have the cash on hand, I can set up a payment plan that deducts a couple hundred dollars from each paycheck. Otherwise, you're fired."

Leon loves his work, and even with the money deducted he'd be making nearly $1,000 a week. What should he do?

Answer to *Paying for a Mistake:*

It's natural for Leon to want to hang onto his job. However, at this point it's unclear whether the engine burn-out was even Jeff's fault, let alone Leon's.

If Leon agreed to pay for a new forklift, though, he'd be accepting the blame—which means he'd be obliged to keep paying even if Bernie had another temper tantrum the next week and decided to fire Leon again.

Plus if the latter happened, Bernie would be able to argue that Leon's admitted negligence should bar him from receiving unemployment checks.

Another consideration is that Bernie has almost certainly insured his forklifts. (If he hasn't, he's more guilty of negligence than Jeff and Leon combined...) That means Bernie's insurance company will reimburse him for the cost of a new vehicle. Bernie's premiums may go up as a result...but not by $15,000. So Bernie's actually asking Leon to hand him a tidy profit on the disaster, by letting him collect on the same destroyed forklift twice.

Leon should walk out the door without accepting even a hint of blame, and be grateful all he lost during this encounter with his unreasonable and greedy employer was his job. That way he won't owe Bernie a dime, and will be able to collect his hard-earned unemployment benefits.

The Petty Manager

Jan loves her job as the hospital where she's worked as a nurse for five years. Unfortunately, her new manager Beatrice is a narrow-minded person who sees people as either "good" or "bad."

After losing a patient, Jan uses some profanity while speaking to another nurse. Beatrice happens to walk by at that moment and overhears. Beatrice tells Jan that if she uses bad words, she must be a bad worker, and she's going to get Jan to leave for the good of the hospital. Jan protests that she has a perfect record, but Beatrice refuses to hear another word and walks off.

Beatrice assigns Jan the most difficult shifts back-to-back. When an exhausted Jan then arrives at work for a shift six minutes late, Beatrice pounces by writing her up for it. Jan is furious at Beatrice's pettiness. Jan signs the write-up in a huff, leaving the "Employee Comments" section blank, and hands it back to Beatrice. Jan hopes this will satisfy Beatrice and exorcise the mean attitude her manager has taken towards her.

Unfortunately, Beatrice is just getting started. A few days later she sends Jan out to find a missing patient. Jan can't locate the patient…and begins to suspect he doesn't even exist. She tells Beatrice that she's looked everywhere and has to give up. Beatrice writes Jan up for failing at her task. This time Jan is so mad that she refuses to even sign the write-up.

The next day HR tells Jan that she's been fired for getting two write-ups within a few days of each other, and for refusing to sign the second write-up.

What should Jan have done differently?

Answer to *The Petty Manager:*

Life is hard when your manager is gunning for you. But at a company where everyone must operate under the same procedures, you can use those rules to your advantage.

Jan's first mistake was to just sign the first write-up. Instead, she should have filled out the "Employee Comments" section and explained her manager had warned that she'd be pursuing a vendetta against Jan…and simply because Jan had gotten upset for a few moments after losing a patient. After writing this and signing it, Jan should have photocopied the write-up before giving it back to Beatrice. This might have caused Beatrice to drop the whole thing and not file the document with HR at all. But at minimum, Jan's documenting Beatrice's harassment creates a foundation for Jan's defense.

Jan's second mistake was refusing to sign a write-up…which is grounds for instant dismissal.

Instead, Jan should have again used the "Employee Comments" section to calmly explain she'd done everything in her power to find the patient, but she didn't know why she was assigned the task because it wasn't even her patient, plus no one she spoke to was aware of such a patient being in the hospital in the first place. She should then have reiterated that her manager had promised to find excuses to run her out of the hospital. Signing and photocopying this second write-up would give HR reason to take the heat off Jan and investigate Beatrice.

Pool of Grievances

Danny works as a pool technician. He likes the work, but he's continually frustrated by his boss Linda.

For example, he doesn't receive a raise at the time Linda said he would. Then when he finally gets the raise, it's not nearly as high as what he'd expected.

Danny also feels picked on. When an unexpected task comes up, Linda calls on Danny to drop what he's doing and take care of it, while his co-workers are allowed to continue their normal assignments.

And while Danny sees his colleagues slacking off, when he takes a lunch break or coffee break Linda often keeps an eye on her watch.

One day Danny returns from the bathroom to have Linda question him about the amount of time he spent there. Annoyed past the breaking point, Danny takes Linda to a spot where no one can hear them and tells her off. He then spends 15 minutes venting to a speechless Linda about everything else she's done that bothers him.

Danny ends with, "If you don't like me working here, why don't you just fire me?"

Linda coldly responds, "If you don't like working here, why don't you leave?"

Feeling he has no choice, Danny does.

How could Danny have handled things better?

Answer to *Pool of Grievances:*

Danny shouldn't have impulsively and angrily confronted his boss with a long series of complaints. That almost guaranteed a bad result.

Danny was right to object to Linda's bathroom interrogation. However, he should've dealt with the other incidents at the time they occurred as well, instead of silently putting up with them until the stress made him blow up.

In addition, Danny should've tried to understand why Linda got along with all her other employees but chose to pick on him. The reason might have been irrational—for example, Danny reminding Linda of an ex-boyfriend. But it's also possible Linda saw Danny as irresponsible, in which case Danny could've taken steps to change that perception.

Finally, if Danny really felt the need to dump a laundry list of grievances on Linda, the way to do so would've been to make an appointment with her at her office, letting her know he needed half an hour to discuss problems at work. This would've given Danny the opportunity to present a calm and carefully organized group of issues—complete with specific examples, and dates and times—and ask that he and Linda work together to resolve them. It also would've demonstrated respect towards Linda, and given her an opportunity to emotionally prepare for the meeting.

Instead, Linda felt off-balance and attacked by Danny's abrupt barrage of complaints—making her response of "Why don't you leave?" virtually inevitable.

No Time Off for Dying Father

For six years, Alice has been one of the most dependable employees of a large department store. Then, unfortunately, her father becomes terminally ill and must be placed in hospice care.

Alice explains the situation to her manager Rick, adding, "I need to temporarily take weekends off so I can care for him."

"Sorry," Rick replies. "That would conflict with store policy, which states full-time employees must always make themselves available to work weekends."

"I know the policy, Rick," says Alice, "but my father is dying and I need to be with him. In six years, I've never taken a sick day. There has to be some way to accommodate me."

"If you need weekends for yourself," Rick responds, "you can change your work status to part-time employee. That'll give you more flexibility."

"It wouldn't be fair to me," Alice points out. "If I switched to part-time, I'd be taking a pay cut of nearly $10 an hour. On top of that, I'd no longer be guaranteed a set number of hours of work each week. Chances are I wouldn't even be able to pay my rent."

"Look, you wanted a solution. That's the best I can do."

"That's no solution, and you know it," Alice says, with tears in her eyes. "Friday will be my last day. I quit."

The next week, Alice applies for unemployment compensation. The store challenges the claim, saying she gave up her benefits when she resigned.

Unwilling to be pushed around any longer, Alice takes the case to court. She tells the judge, "Your Honor, Rick forced me to leave. The only alternatives he gave me were to accept a demotion that wouldn't allow me to pay my bills, or to abandon my sick father to die alone."

"She had another choice, your Honor," Rick counters. "She could've requested time off under FMLA, the Family and Medical Leave Act."

Alice is shocked. "I've never heard of that!" she protests. "Rick never mentioned it as an option."

"I didn't have to," Rick says. "The information is in the company handbook, which all employees are supposed to read."

Will the judge side with Rick or Alice?

Answer to *No Time Off for Dying Father:*

The judge will rule for Alice.

When Alice explained her situation to Rick, it was his responsibility under Federal law to inform her of her eligibility to take some time off under FMLA. Instead, the only option he gave Alice was a cost-prohibitive demotion to a part-time job.

Rick's actions were not only heartless, but illegal. And it's precisely this kind of inhumane behavior that FMLA is designed to prevent.

Safety First

Richard is a conscientious welder, but he's having a rough time working for his employer Dan. Dan has a fiery temper; but even worse, Dan seems to feel safety is a luxury. At least once a week there aren't enough welding gloves available, and Dan tells Richard to work without one, saying "Just pay attention and you'll be fine." Richard responds by buying his own gloves, which he carries to and from work every day.

Dan is also lax in checking and maintaining cables and hoses, making Richard feel like he's working in a war zone where something could blow up any second.

One day Richard comes to work and finds there aren't enough welding helmets to go around. Richard explains the situation to Dan, who replies, "Okay, I'll have more helmets in next week. But in the meantime work without one. If you're careful, you'll be fine."

Richard shakes his head. "I could be blinded by the intensity of the flame. Or a piece of metal could shoot into my face."

Dan says, "I'm hiring men, not babies. Get the work done if you want to keep your job. If you refuse, it'll be the same as quitting."

What should Richard do?

Answer to *Safety First:*

Richard should say, "I'm not quitting, but you're asking me to violate standard safety protocols. I can do other work for you today that doesn't put me in extreme danger, so I'll stick around for that unless you order me to leave." As long as Richard doesn't walk off and expresses willingness to do other work, Dan can't claim that Richard quit.

After work, Richard should file a complaint with the US Occupational Safety and Health Administration (see Web site http://www.osha.gov/as/opa/worker/index.html). It's against the law for Dan to fire, transfer, or in any other way punish Richard for doing this; and OSHA can help ensure Dan takes safety at his company more seriously, which will help not only Richard but all of his co-workers.

Missing the Forest for the Trees

Jack climbs tall trees and prunes their branches using a chain saw. It's a dangerous occupation, but Jack loves being outdoors and working with nature.

While high up in a tree one day, Jack comes across a bird's nest with five baby birds in it. It's initially a sweet moment. But then a protective mother bird who's been hovering unseen above flies at Jack and claws at his face! Jack is so startled that he loses his balance. His safety belt snaps taut to save him...but then breaks!

Jack plummets down the side of the tree trunk for 40 feet. He's knocked unconscious even before he lands. Jack wakes up in a hospital room, where he's told that he has a concussion, a broken rib, and 19 knocked-out teeth, and is lucky to be alive.

Jack's employer PruneCo subscribes to worker's compensation insurance, and that pays for most of Jack's medical bills. It doesn't cover Jack's pain and suffering, though. Plus Jack's doctor forbids him from any more tree climbing, which means he needs to find a new job. Jack therefore hires a worker's compensation attorney to get him more money.

After just a month, Jack's lawyer negotiates a settlement with PruneCo that Jack is happy to accept. Jack is also happy that he's sufficiently recovered to begin looking for a new position—though this time telecommuting from his home computer. But Jack doesn't know how long it'll take to be hired for a new occupation, so he files for unemployment.

PruneCo challenges Jack's claim, and both parties end up in unemployment court. The judge is sympathetic as Jack tells his story. Then PruneCo's attorney Mr. Turner examines Jack.

"Do you recall signing a Worker's Compensation Agreement as a result of your injury?" Turner asks. "Yes," says Jack.

"Is this the Agreement?" Turner asks. Jack flips through the pages and says, "Yes, it is."

"You were represented by counsel, correct?" Jack again answers "Yes."

"Do you see page 2 of the agreement where it states *In consideration of the settlement for this worker's compensation claim, I voluntarily resign*? And is that your signature at the bottom?"

Jack stares at the page. He's speechless.

What can Jack do?

Answer to *Missing the Forest for the Trees:*

Unless Jack has a time machine that lets him return to the past and hire a different attorney, all he can do is give up.

Jack's workman's compensation lawyer was focused on getting a quick settlement instead of looking at the big picture and taking into account all of Jack's needs. This narrow approach ended up costing Jack thousands of dollars in unemployment benefits.

It should be noted that the judge would consider whether the employee was unable to perform their job at the time of separation and for the foreseeable future. If a worker cannot physically continue to work, the signing of a workers' compensation settlement agreement is not controlling in determining whether the separation occurred under disqualifying circumstances. If the employee had ongoing medical restrictions that would prevent him/her from returning to their regular duties and/or pay in the foreseeable future, their decision to sign the settlement agreement does not obviate the fact that the employee could not physically return to his/her normal job. If the employee is unable to continue with their work, then the voluntary resignation would be attributable to an illness or injury, requiring separation from the employment. The other issue to consider is whether the employer would have permitted the employee to return to their pre-injury job if they had refused its workers' compensation settlement offer.

"Double-Bolt Your Door"

Jon is the secretary for a New York attorney named Frank. When Jon took the job, he was excited to be working in a fancy Manhattan law office. To his surprise and dismay, though, he must continually deal with calls from furious clients. When Jon has to tell them Frank isn't available, they often respond with yelling, or worse.

For example, one caller begins with, "Where's your boss, I need to talk to him now!"

"Well, er," Jon stammers, "he should be in, uh, later today. Can I take a message?"

"Listen, jerk," the client responds, "you already have 50 messages from me and none of them have been returned!"

"Oh," Jon says, "I'm, ah, really sorry that—"

"We're beyond apologies!" screams the client. "Frank has my money! If I don't hear from him by 5:00 pm, he better watch his back. And I suggest you double-bolt your door at night too!"

After calls like this from over a dozen clients, Jon fears for his safety.

He conducts some research on his own time and learns that Frank is under investigation by the Attorney Generals of at least three US states.

Deeply concerned, Jon pokes around office files. He finds some evidence indicating Frank is engaged in taking payroll funds from trust and escrow accounts illegally.

So in addition to worrying about his physical well-being, Jon is now terrified he'll end up in jail.

Feeling like he'll suffocate if he's in the office another moment, Jon stands up from his desk, gathers his things, and walks out of the office, locking it behind him. And he never returns.

Did Jon do the right thing, or should he have first discussed his concerns with Frank?

Answer to *"Double-Bolt Your Door:"*

You should normally let your employer know about problems and offer a reasonable opportunity to address them before quitting. And if that doesn't work out, it's standard to give two weeks notice.

However, when an employer is breaking the law, or engaged in some other behavior that reasonable people would consider heinous, it's fine to quit without notification.

Jon had cause to fear for his life from Frank's *clients*, so there's no telling what sort of danger Frank himself might have posed to a witness of his illegal activities.

Jon did the right thing. In fact, his fleeing the office happened in the nick of time—the police arrested Frank just a week later. They later questioned Jon as a possible accomplice, but because he'd quit they eliminated him as a suspect.

A Gag Blows Up

Gary is an assembly worker at a large parts distribution company. His colleagues consider him a jokester who'll do anything for a laugh.

One day Gary is feeling especially playful when he spots an empty plastic water bottle. To the amusement of his co-workers, he attaches a high pressure hose to the spout and pumps air until the bottle loudly pops. This gets a big laugh from everyone—except Gary's supervisor Tracy, who happens to walk in unnoticed towards the end.

Tracy goes up to Gary and demands, "What the hell are you doing?"

"I just wanted to see what would happen," says Gary, chuckling. "All the guys got a kick out of it."

"Don't you know how dangerous it is to create an explosion around all this equipment?" asks Tracy. "Don't you realize that you might've propelled plastic or metal into someone's face?"

Gary looks at the ground. "No, I didn't think of it."

"Well, then," says Tracy, "let me give you plenty of time to do that. You're fired."

Gary is shocked. "I was just kidding around!" he protests. "It helps everybody feel good. Okay, I used bad judgment just now. But I'm sorry, and I won't do it again."

Tracy looks Gary straight in the eyes. "You'll never have the chance. Get your stuff and leave immediately."

Did Tracy overreact, or did he do the right thing?

Answer to *A Gag Blows Up:*

Tracy had little choice about firing Gary. Virtually any large company has rules—spelled out in the employee handbook—prohibiting actions that violate the safety of its workers.

Also, Gary's excuse of "bad judgment" doesn't hold up because under labor law that refers to a worker having to pick among multiple actions and making an inferior choice. That doesn't fit this situation, in which Gary never had a work-related need to create the safety violation.

Further, Gary's company will successfully block his claim for unemployment benefits because he deliberately disregarded his duties to his employer, which is the definition of misconduct under labor law.

With no job and zero benefits, Gary was no longer chuckling.

After several hard months, Gary finally found work again; and from that point on he restricted his comedy tools to verbal humor and fart noises, neither of which are prohibited in the handbook.

Cheating Hearts

Morty owns a large jewelry store. Although Morty is married, he has a well-known habit of flirting with the women who come by.

Morty doesn't always stop at flirting, either—it's an open secret he's having an affair with Linda, the owner of a shop around the corner. Morty's employees are baffled by this, as Linda is a very plain-looking woman, while Morty's wife Carrie is gorgeous.

Carrie comes by the jewelry store periodically looking for Morty. More and more, she doesn't find him because he's off somewhere with Linda. Carrie eventually figures out what's going on…and she turns to Donald, who is Morty's top salesman, to be consoled.

After a few weeks, Donald's consoling turns increasingly intense and romantic. He begins to buy Carrie gifts. It starts with flowers and candy. That escalates to lingerie and dresses.

As the relationship continues, Donald feels compelled to offer Carrie presents he can't afford. He removes a diamond bracelet from the store and gives it to Carrie.

Donald rationalizes that it's not really stealing because she's Morty's wife and Morty owns the store.

Carrie wears the bracelet, and Morty naturally notices. He questions Carrie, and she replies, "You don't buy me presents, so I bought one for myself."

A few weeks later, Carrie wears a Piaget watch. Morty again notices and questions her. This time Carrie's response is vague and she quickly changes the subject.

A suspicious Morty checks his inventory and discovers that his store is missing the watch and the diamond bracelet—and also a pair of gold earrings and a diamond necklace! He returns home at a time when he knows Carrie won't be there, and he discovers all these items in her jewelry box.

After the store closes, Morty asks Donald to stick around. Morty asks, "Are you having an affair with my wife?" Donald shakes with apprehension. He confesses to Morty, saying "I wanted to end it, but just couldn't find the strength." Morty calmly continues, "You've been giving Carrie gifts taken from the store, haven't you?" Donald says, "Yes. I'm really sorry. I know it was wrong."

To Donald's great surprise, Morty responds, "Don't worry about it. As you know, I haven't exactly been loyal myself." While a shocked Donald stands with his jaw open, Morty adds, "Just try to not give the whole store away."

Should Donald relax?

Answer to *Cheating Hearts:*

No. Donald is living on borrowed time.

After two more months, Morty's relationship with Linda ends. The very next day, Morty fires Donald for stealing.

Donald is lucky Morty doesn't also press charges with the police...

Don't steal from your employer, for any reason.

And don't mess around with your boss' spouse.

I Kissed the Sheriff

Laurie has worked 12 years as a deputy sheriff. It's a stressful job, and so she especially loves letting off steam at the annual Christmas party.

The festivities are held at a local restaurant, with all the officers in plain clothes. After a couple of hours of drinking, Laurie starts chatting at the bar with her fellow deputy sheriff Richard. The conversation slowly turns flirtatious. Laurie puts her arms around Richard and pulls him toward her for a kiss. This turns into an extended make-out session.

Their boss, Captain Mahoney, is visibly annoyed by the public display of affection. Laurie and Richard don't notice because they're so focused on each other.

However, the next day when Laurie arrives at the station, the Captain calls her into his office. Laurie enters and asks, "What's up?"

"I'm not happy about your behavior at the Christmas party," the Captain says. "I thought what you and Richard did was conduct unbecoming of deputies. I'm suspending you. And when he comes in, I'm suspending Richard too."

Laurie is shocked. "We were off duty, sir. And it was a party. The whole point was to relax."

"I'm sorry," replies the Captain, "but there are limits, and you exceeded them. You're suspended for a month without pay."

Who's right?

Answer to *I Kissed the Sheriff:*

This is a case where it almost doesn't matter who's right. Even if the Captain is overreacting, Laurie should've considered how others might view her behavior.

As long as you're in the presence of your fellow workers—and especially your boss—it's important to maintain your professionalism. Otherwise you may say or do something that becomes the fodder of water cooler conversation for months afterwards...and permanently change how your employer perceives you.

That's doubly true for someone like Laurie, who as a law enforcement office must adhere to a higher standard because she's representing the entire police department. While Laurie was out of uniform at the party, she's a beat cop known by virtually everyone in the neighborhood.

Another example of this is a UPS delivery man who went to a strip bar during his lunch hour. He was fired because he was still in uniform, and so his being at the club risked creating a public perception that UPS endorsed his off-hour activity.

Regardless of whether you're in or out of the office, you should always be aware of what kinds of perceptions you're creating—and how they might reflect on your employer.

A Unique Use of the Employee Discount

Gary works in the parts department at a BMW car dealership. He's paid a very good salary, and his duties seem straightforward: continually audit the inventory to make sure what's on the shelves and what's in the computer database match up.

That may sound like a simple task...but it isn't. For example, Gary receives a shipment with an invoice stating it includes 1,000 light bulbs, but in reality has only 992 bulbs. Gary can't spend all day counting bulbs, so he has to accept the invoice number and then account for any discrepancy later on.

As another example, the dealership's salespeople regularly take items off the shelves without Gary's knowledge and give them to their customers to build loyalty. It's a good investment for the company, but it messes up Gary's accounting.

In addition, items that upon examination prove to be defective are often thrown away behind Gary's back.

Because of such "wild card" factors, the inventory on the shelves never precisely matches what's in the database. And even though it's not Gary's fault, whenever his manager happens to notice a discrepancy he yells, screams and threatens to take away Gary's job.

Gary is faced with an impossible situation...and considering the heat of his last reprimand, he feels sure that next time he'll be fired. This inspired Gary to come up with a unique solution.

Whenever Gary discovers a shortage of parts, he purchases those missing parts himself using his employee discount!

This may seem ridiculous. However, the cost of most of the parts is insignificant compared to what Gary earns each week.

The only potential problem is that the company's discount policy flatly states that the parts are for the employee's personal use only. But Gary reasons that there's no more personal use for these parts than to have them save his job...

Gary's system works for six entire months. The physical and database inventories remain matched up, and there are no further reprimands.

Then one day Gary's manager happens to notice an invoice for two BMW thermostats addressed to Gary. His manager knows Gary doesn't own a BMW, so he questions Gary about the purchase. Gary has no choice but to reveal what he's been doing.

Gary's manager fires him on the spot, saying that Gary's violated the company's rules for employee discounts.

Who's right?

Answer to *A Unique Use of the Employee Discount:*

Gary and his manager are both partially right.

Gary came up with an oddly ingenious solution to an impossible problem created by his thick-headed manager. What his manager should've done instead of yelling at Gary is work to understand the issues Gary was dealing with and find reasonable ways for Gary to resolve inventory discrepancies.

At the same time, Gary really did violate the employee discount policy. In this context, "personal use" means that the employee purchases the item to use himself, not as a gift for someone else or on behalf of someone else. When an employee does the latter, the company considers it theft...which is grounds for both dismissal and denial of unemployment benefits.

The twist here is that the "gifts" Gary was purchasing were for the company itself! So while he technically violated company policy, an unemployment judge is unlikely to consider Gary's actions rising to the level of misconduct worthy of denial of benefits. That's especially true considering Gary received zero warnings—when his manager found out what was happening, he fired Gary instantly.

One other twist is that if Gary had purchased the items at full price—that is, without using his employee discount—then there might not have been any grounds for firing him.

Blood Rules

Tiffany draws blood from patients for medical lab tests. She handles dozens of patients a day, and takes pride in how meticulous she is in labeling and processing blood samples.

Conversely, her supervisor Harold is shockingly sloppy. It's Harold's job to double-check the work of all the other technicians for accuracy, but Tiffany has run across and corrected over a dozen errors he's committed. Whenever she points one out to him, Harold coldly responds, "Last time I checked, I'm the supervisor here. Just do your job and don't worry about mine."

Fearing for both the safety of patients and lawsuits that could destroy the company, Tiffany decides she can't stay quiet any longer. She makes an appointment with Pamela, the head of her company's HR department, and lays out all her concerns.

Pamela listens intently until Tiffany is done, and then says, "I thank you for bringing this to my attention, and I take it seriously. However, you're telling me that Harold will deny everything, which leaves us with your word against his. I need concrete proof that all these blunders occurred."

"Oh, I've got proof," declares Tiffany. "It's in my car. I'll be right back." Tiffany runs out, and then returns a few minutes later with three vials of blood labeled with patient names and birthdates.

Tiffany is feeling great at the opportunity to finally present her evidence—but Pamela is appalled. "Tiffany, what have you done?! Patient samples aren't supposed to leave the lab at any time, under any circumstances. You've violated Federal HIPAA law. And you've given me no choice but to terminate your employment, effective immediately."

Is this a shocking case of injustice?

Answer to *"Blood Rules:"*

This is a complicated situation in which everyone did something wrong.

The worst offender is Harold, whose carelessness and indifference is endangering patients who might not get the critical treatment they need because of mislabeled blood samples. Harold is also endangering the future of his company, since even a single death resulting from his incompetence could result in a lawsuit that bankrupts the firm.

As for Pamela, she should be actively encouraging whistleblowers such as Tiffany. But instead of focusing on the patient lives at risk, Pamela is fixating on Tiffany's potential violation of the 1996 Health Insurance Portability and Accountability Act (HIPAA), which forbids actions that would allow patient data to be made public. Tiffany removing blood samples from the lab and leaving them in her car created the possibility of their information being released—for example, by someone breaking into the car and stealing them.

Given the reason behind Tiffany's action, though, and the fact that the samples had not actually strayed beyond the company, Pamela could've cut Tiffany some slack.

That said, a company is entitled to interpret HIPAA strictly. And there are other ways Tiffany could've provided evidence of Harold's negligence, such as documenting each error in a journal and taking photographs. It may seem grossly unfair that a woman trying to save lives gets fired for it. But the point is that Tiffany should've known the rules of her profession, and her company's interpretation of those rules, and abided by them. If Tiffany cared deeply about helping patients, she should've avoided a reckless act that not only cost her job, but damaged the chances of her being believed over her boss.

Broadway Vacation

Matt maintains the soda vending machines for a string of offices in Florida. Nobody in his company thinks of Matt as a cultured guy, but he and his wife are actually huge theatre buffs. The highlight of their year is his summer vacation, when they fly out to New York for two weeks and see a Broadway show every night.

Matt doesn't make a high salary, though, so the only way he can afford this treat is to plan ahead and pay for everything at heavily discounted prices.

In May, Matt asks his manager if going on vacation the first week of July will be okay. His manager replies, "That's fine with me. I'll pass it along to HR."

A month goes by and Matt hears nothing else about it, so he assumes his request is approved. Matt goes on the Web and finds great deals for plane tickets, Broadway tickets, and a hotel room. All these purchases are nonrefundable, but that doesn't concern Matt because he's committed to the trip.

The next day Matt comes to work and finds his vacation request returned from HR with the word

"Denied" written on top. He rushes to his manager and asks, "What's going on?"

"Two other workers requested vacations before you did for the same week," his manager replies. "Your being gone would leave us short-handed. You'll have to pick another vacation date."

Matt shakes his head in a daze. "I submitted this request a month ago and you told me it was fine. I've already spent thousands of dollars—all my vacation money—on tickets that can't be returned!"

I'm really sorry," his manager replies. "But if you don't show up for work the first week in July, I'll have to fire you."

What should Matt do?

Answer to *Broadway Vacation:*

Matt should pull out his employee manual—or visit it on his company's Web site—and carefully study its rules regarding vacations.

If the manual says vacations can be approved verbally by his manager, then Matt can go to HR and make a strong case that the denial is meaningless because he'd already received a green light for it—and had made commitments based on that okay.

If the manual says vacations must be approved in writing, however, then Matt is out of luck. He should have asked his manager—or better yet, HR—to get back to him as soon as possible so he could perform the planning his vacation required.

The lesson here is to be crystal clear about your company's vacation policies. And whenever in doubt, get the approval for your vacation in writing.

The Dirty Chicken

Jim runs the deli counter, and he loves his job. First thing every Tuesday morning Dorothy comes in for a chicken. Jim exchanges pleasantries, telling Dorothy there's a special on roast beef if she's interested. "No," Dorothy says, "the chicken is all I want." Jim smiles and begins to wrap it up—when the slippery chicken slips from his hands and falls on the floor. "Darn it," says Jim. "So much for that bird. I can't sell it now."

"Can't you just wash it?" asks Dorothy. "I could," says Jim, "but it's against store policy. Once it touches the ground, it's considered garbage."

"That's too bad," says Dorothy. "Your morning floor is as shiny and clean as a dinner plate. It seems like a waste of good poultry."

Jim nods. "I agree, but those are the rules. Anyway, let me get you another chicken." Jim does so, and Dorothy leaves happy. But her words stay with him. *The chicken is officially garbage now,* Jim thinks. *Why don't I take it home with me and have it for supper tonight?*

Jim washes the chicken, wraps it up, writes his name on the wrapping paper, and places it in the refrigerator.

At the end of the day, Jim retrieves the chicken and puts it in his knapsack. His manger happens to notice, but says nothing. As soon as Jim steps out of the store, however, the manager rushes after Jim and says, "Wait a second. What's that bulge in your knapsack?"

"I'm taking home a chicken that fell on the ground," Jim replies.

"Do you have a receipt for it?" asks his manager.

"No," says Jim. "I didn't buy it. No one can. That would be against store policy."

"So is stealing," his manager replies. "You're a good worker, Jim, but our company has strong rules about theft. I'm afraid I have to let you go."

"You can't fire me for taking away garbage!" Jim exclaims.

Is Jim right?

Answer to *The Dirty Chicken:*

Jim is wrong.

Even though the chicken is officially garbage, it's *his company's* garbage—that is, it belongs to the store as long as it remains within the store's property. Jim has no right to take it home without getting his manager's permission…which is what he should've asked for.

If this seems like an arbitrary policy, consider a scenario in which Jim meant to steal the chicken all along. When his manager catches him putting it into his knapsack, Jim replies, "Oh, it fell on the ground, so it's okay for me to take it." How can his manager know if it really fell? And even if it did, how can his manager know Jim didn't drop it deliberately so he could take it home for free? The company would be creating an incentive for employees to have frequent "accidents" with its food.

After his manager explains this, Jim begs forgiveness and swears it'll never happen again; and he provides Dorothy's phone number so she can confirm the chicken really was dropped. The manager lets Jim go with a warning. However, a lot of other workers caught trying to take home company property aren't as lucky.

Presumed Guilty

Rose has worked as a cashier for a large department store for four years. One day as the store's about to close she spills coffee on her blouse. She decides to change by taking one of the store's t-shirts and ringing the purchase up on her register. She then goes into one of the changing room and makes the swap.

A few days later, a man Rose has never seen before approaches her and says, "You have to come with me." Rose looks at him. "Excuse me? Who are you?" The man flashes an ID card at Rose and says, "I'm Mr. Rushup, store security. Let's talk in private."

He leads her to a back room of the store Rose has never seen before, but has heard about. It's where shoplifters are interrogated.

After they sit down, Rose says, "What's this about?" Rushup says flatly, "This store has had a rash of after-hour thefts lately, and I've been brought in from the main office to stop it. I think you're the culprit, so you're being discharged."

"I've been a loyal employee for years without a blemish on my record," Rose protests. "I haven't done anything wrong!"

"I've been reviewing surveillance tapes, and it looks like you have. Are there any items you removed from the store recently?"

"I bought a t-shirt three days ago."

"Do you have the receipt?"

"It cost only $4.99, and it's not tax deductible. Of course I didn't keep the receipt."

"That's too bad, because the store is prepared to press charges."

"You've got to be kidding! You're going to prosecute me for buying a t-shirt?"

"It's your word against the surveillance tape. But I see a way out of this for you. If you want to keep working as a cashier, admit in writing what you did."

"Write that I purchased a t-shirt?"

"No!" Rushup roars. "Admit that you stole store merchandise! It's your only chance."

Rose hesitates; but she's intimidated by Rushup, and she wants to keep her job. Rose writes that she stole the t-shirt and signs her name.

Rushup grabs the sheet of paper and quickly exits the room, leaving Rose to sit alone and wonder what's going on.

Ten minutes later, Rose's manager comes in. "Rose," he says, "we've gathered your personal effects. Security is going to escort you out of the store."

"What?!" says Rose. "Mr. Rushup said if I did what he said, I could keep working."

"You can," her manager replies, "but not for this store. And also not for any other store owned by our company. You've been fired, and blackballed as a thief."

What was Rose's big mistake?

Answer to *Presumed Guilty:*

Rose should never have trusted Mr. Rushup.

When an outsider is brought in to stop internal theft, he doesn't necessarily care about catching the person who's doing it. In many cases, his goal is to point the blame at *someone* as quickly as possible. This makes the investigator look good; and it sends a strong message to the real crook to stop stealing. So even if the wrong person is fired, the thefts are likely to end for a while…making it appear the investigator chose wisely.

And the investigator feels no remorse, rationalizing that if an employee signs a confession, he or she must be guilty of *something*…

If Rose had simply stuck to her guns about her innocence, the store could never have proven she'd done anything wrong. The surveillance tape merely showed that Rose took the shirt…which she readily admitted. The tape did *not* prove she failed to pay for the shirt.

But even if Rose was fired based on suspicion alone, she would've definitely been entitled to unemployment benefits.

As is, the store will use her confession to prevent Rose from collecting benefits.

off the mark.com
by Mark Parisi
HELLO, BOSS?...I'M ENJOYING MY SHOWER ENTIRELY TOO MUCH, SO I DON'T SEE HOW I COULD MAKE IT IN BEFORE 10:30...
offthemark.com
ATLANTIC FEATURE © 1992 MARK PARISI
MARK PARISI

Late Kate

Kate is an assistant at Dr. Stevens' medical practice. She's supposed to arrive for work at 8:30 am. Recently she's been spending a lot of nights with her hot new boyfriend, though, which often delays her getting to the office until around 8:40 am.

The lateness is minor enough to not attract Dr. Stevens' attention for weeks. One morning Kate doesn't show until 9:05 am, though, which spurs him to ask his bookkeeper if she has any idea how often Kate fails to arrive on time. The bookkeeper estimates it happens every other day—that is, 15 times in the last month. Dr. Stevens is shocked at the frequency of the problem.

Dr. Stevens calls Kate into his office and tells her that her behavior is unacceptable. "You have to do better," he says. "Everyone else manages to get here on time." Kate apologizes, and she promises to improve.

For two weeks, Kate arrives at the office like clockwork.

But then one day she shows up at 8:35…five minutes late.

Dr. Stevens calls her into his office again. "I warned you a couple weeks ago about this," he says. "I can't tolerate your tardiness any longer. Today will be your last day."

Kate is stunned. "You can't do this! I called in at 8:00 am and notified your service that I had a flat tire. It's a small miracle that I was only five minutes late."

"I don't care," Dr. Stevens responds. "Your attendance record is atrocious. I gave you one more chance, and you blew it. Please gather your things and leave."

"It's not fair," says Kate.

"If you don't like that, you'll hate this: Because of your frequent misconduct, I'll be fighting you on unemployment benefits."

Will Dr. Stevens manage to avoid paying for Kate's unemployment?

Answer to *Late Kate:*

Dr. Stevens is free to fire Kate, but that's as far it goes.

It's true that Kate had a terrible attendance record. But to successfully challenge Kate's unemployment benefits, Dr. Stevens must prove misconduct.

Dr. Stevens didn't warn Kate about her lateness for a long time, which means his attendance policy was vague. And when he finally did warn her, he used mild language, simply saying "You have to do better," so Kate had no idea that one more lateness would cause her to be fired.

Further, Dr. Stevens never questioned Kate about her previous instances of lateness, so he has no way to determine if the causes for them are reasonable or not. The only lateness for which Dr. Stevens knows the full story is Kate's most recent one—and in that case she had an entirely legitimate reason by way of a flat tire. Plus she behaved responsibly, calling into the office to say she'd be late, and arriving only five minutes tardy. None of that comes close to rising to the level of misconduct.

Time Sheet Cheat

Joe is an employee of Watching You Corporation (WYC), a service that supplies security guards by the hour. Joe's current assignment is the midnight to 8:00 am shift at New York's Port Authority. Joe enjoys the robust energy of the location and the variety of people who pass through. He also likes his dock manager Fred, a laid-back old-timer who lets Joe leave a half hour early when he's not really needed.

Unfortunately for Joe, the head of operations at Port Authority notices several times when Joe leaves his post at 7:30 am, and he informs WYC that they're overbilling for Joe's services.

Joe's WYC supervisor Richard therefore calls him in. "I've been looking at your time card," Richard begins, "and it doesn't match up with your time sheet. Why is that?"

"It's because Fred is easy-going," Joe replies. "There are days when things are slow, or when someone else shows up early, and I'm not really needed. Since there's no point to my being there at those times, Fred lets me leave early to beat the rush hour commute."

"You make that sound very reasonable," says Richard. "You know what else is reasonable? You're fired. And don't even try applying for unemployment benefits, because you don't have a prayer of getting them."

Is Richard right?

Answer to *Time Sheet Cheat:*

Richard did the right thing. He's also correct that Joe's actions make himself ineligible for unemployment benefits.

Fred giving Joe permission to leave early means Joe did nothing wrong in working fewer hours. However, he should've accurately reported those fewer hours on his timesheet to WYC. By claiming more time than he actually worked, Joe lied to his employer and committed theft by overcharging Port Authority.

Joe can't excuse his actions by pointing to his dock manager, because Fred didn't have the authority to okay Joe billing for hours he didn't work. If Joe had any confusion about this, he should've discussed it with Richard. Since he didn't, his dishonest acts mandated termination.

Drug Test Dilemma

George had been waiting months for the Rolling Stones reunion tour to come to his town. The night of the concert, everybody in the arena is going nuts. Sitting next to George are some very festive and friendly rockers. After the first song, they pass a joint over. George hasn't touched drugs since college, but for nostalgia's sake he takes a quick hit before passing it back to them with a nod of thanks and a motion saying, "I'm good."

A week later at work, George gets a memo that he's among the "winners" of that day's random drug testing, and he should report immediately to the clinic to provide a urine sample.

George has been through this routine in the past and never worried about it. But now his experience at the rock concert flashes through his mind. He took that hit of pot. What if this costs him his job?

George considers going straight to HR and explaining what happened at the concert. *If I'm just honest,* he thinks, *they probably won't fire me.*

What should George do?

Answer to *Drug Test Dilemma:*

If George admits to smoking the pot, there's a strong chance he'll be fired on the spot. A company serious enough about drugs to regularly enforce random spot testing is likely to have a zero tolerance policy.

That wouldn't serve the truth in this case, however, because George is actually drug free. And it wouldn't be good for either him or his company to end his job over a moment of weakness.

Instead, before the test George should drink as much water as he can and urinate as much as he can to dilute whatever pot might still be in his system—and then simply take the test and see what happens.

It's quite possible George's body has flushed the chemicals from that single hit after a week, or that what remains will be too small for the test to pick up. In these cases, George is home free.

Then again, if George tests positive, the amount found will be so weak that he can claim it's the result of breathing the air around a crowd full of pot-smokers at last week's big concert—which is sort of true.

As a last resort, George can hire an attorney to challenge the evidence. A lot of drug testing companies aren't rigorous about how they handle samples, and/or skip obtaining the necessary Federal approval to conduct official testing in the first place, so a good lawyer can often get a court to set aside the results of the test.

George loses nothing by getting tested and awaiting the results—while if he confesses, the odds are he'll be fired instantly—and lose his unemployment to boot. So this is a case where honesty isn't really the best policy...especially since the "bigger truth" is that George isn't really a drug user.

Employee Intervention

Ian is a middle-aged bachelor who owns a publishing company. Ian normally arrives at work every day in a suit and tie, with well-manicured nails and neatly combed hair, and behaves with calm reserve.

Over the last month, however, Ian's come to work with no tie, terribly long nails, and hair that looks like it's never washed, let alone combed. And he increasingly loses his temper and screams at his employees, who are Louise, Betty, and Sophie.

One day after Ian leaves early, the senior staffer Louise asks Betty and Sophie to a meeting. She begins with, "Do you have any idea what's going on with Ian?"

"I'm really glad you brought this up," says Betty. "Last week he couldn't find the Wite-Out and he acted as if he'd lost a million dollars."

Sophie nods. "A few days ago, he got so mad at a customer that he threw a book across the room. It nearly hit me in the head. I didn't say anything, but I was really scared."

"He's forgetful too," adds Louise. "On Monday he told me to write a check to Austin Paper. Yesterday I asked him to sign it, and he told me the check should actually go to Houston Ink. And he made it sound like I'm the one who made the mistake."

"I really like working here," says Sophie, "but if something isn't done the company will go under."

"Do you have any suggestions?" asks Louise.

"Yeah," replies Betty. "Let's get Ian to take a drug test."

"That's not a bad idea," says Louise. "The company handbook requires periodic testing of employees."

Sophie shakes her head. "Ian's not an employee, he's the owner!"

"No," says Betty. "Technically, Ian's an employee of the company just as much as we are."

"But how do we get him to go along?" asks Sophie.

"I'll take care of that," says Louise.

The next day Louise approaches her boss. "Ian, our car insurance company is requiring all employees to take a drug test."

Ian motions dismissively and says, "Fine, get it done."

"Okay," says Louise. "That includes you, by the way."

Ian stops and looks apprehensive. "What do you mean!? I'm the boss!!"

"I know," Louise continues. "But they're going by the corporate records, which lists you as an employee. We all have to do it or we'll lose the insurance."

Ian mumbles to himself, and Louise leaves.

A few days later a registered technician comes to the office and administers the drug tests to everyone, including Ian.

Did Louise cross a line she shouldn't have?

Answer to *Employee Intervention:*

While it's not normally okay to lie to your boss, this was a case where the fate of the entire company was at risk. Louise did what she and the rest of the staff felt was in the best interests of everyone.

When the test results came back, they showed the staff has passed...but Ian failed. Louise, Betty and Sophie weren't shocked by that. However, they *were* surprised at the reason: Ian's urine sample wasn't from a person, but from a dog!

Louise, Betty, and Sophie approached Ian together with the test results and encouraged him to go into rehab.

After some initial reluctance, Ian did.

This ended up saving the company...and everyone's jobs.

U R an Idi0t

Jim is a graphic artist at a monthly sports magazine. He and his manager Brad are both football fans, and they develop a friendly rivalry about who is better at predicting winners.

At first, whoever chooses the right team simply gets to text a gloating message seconds after the game ends to the guy who guessed wrong.

After a while, though, Brad suggests they put some money on the line "to make it more interesting." Jim is fine with that, so they each start betting $200 against the other's pick, with the winner texting "U R a Loser" after the game and collecting the cash the next morning.

This remains cordial while each of them is guessing right about half the time. As the season goes on, though, Jim's percentage of accurate picks increases, making Brad slowly but surely more testy.

A month before Super Bowl Sunday, while Brad is paying Jim off he says, "You're on a helluva streak. Any chance you're getting inside information from my reporters?"

"They would never do that to you," Jim replies, grinning. "Besides, their guess is as good as ours. I've just been lucky."

Jim gets the next three bets right. While he tries to not show it, Brad is steaming. He quietly interviews each of his reporters about who they believe will win the Super Bowl, claiming it is information the magazine might use for an article. Brad also spends days studying stats and reading game analyses on the Web.

At the end of work on Friday, Brad calls Jim into his office and says as casually as he can manage, "You know, this weekend's Super Bowl is special. We should make an extra special bet for it."

Jim innocently asks, "What do you have in mind?"

Brad says, "How about $2,000? That's what you've won from me. So this would be my chance to break even, or for you to double up."

Jim is taken aback. "Wow, that's serious money. Whoever chooses wrong might become pretty upset."

"Don't be ridiculous," Brad says. "We're both grown men. Besides, what's the point of working on a sports magazine if you can't be a good loser?"

Jim isn't happy, but he senses his job is at risk if he refuses. "Okay," he says. "You're on." Brad picks the championship team all his sources say will win. Jim is fine with that, saying, "I can't explain it, but I have a good feeling about the challenger."

That Sunday, the underdog team scores one of the biggest upsets in Super Bowl history.

Jim is ecstatic. He spends the night dreaming about all the ways he can spend his windfall $2,000.

When Jim returns to work on Monday, he notices his name is missing from his parking spot. Then when he swipes his office badge to enter the building, the door doesn't open. Jim calls the office receptionist on his cell and asks what's going on.

"Gee," she says, "Brad told us you quit."

"How could I have quit when I haven't even been in the office yet?"

"Brad said you texted him after your team pick lost the Super Bowl. He says you wrote, 'FU and your GD bets. U R an Idi0t. Ciao 4ever to U and your job.'"

"My pick *won* the Super Bowl!" Jim shouts. "That jerk is trying to get out of paying two grand."

"Jim, I believe you," says the receptionist. "So will everyone else who's worked closely with you. But Brad has seniority, and the bosses are going to take his word over yours."

That proves to be true. Further, the magazine fights Jim when he applies for unemployment benefits, saying he quit.

Who will win?

Answer to *U R an Idi0t:*

Since the top executives at Jim's magazine trust Brad over him, Jim can't save his job.

However, Jim wins his unemployment benefits. The fact that he came to the office as usual Monday morning shows he was ready to continue working. As for the text message Brad claims to have received, it's legally considered "hearsay." That means it can be used to supplement other evidence, but by itself has no weight unless Brad produces the actual message and proves it came from Jim—which, of course, he can't.

On his next job, Jim refrains from making "friendly" bets with his boss. He also lets it be widely known that Brad is a welcher—which ends up making Brad an outcast in the sports community when, a year later, his magazine folds due to poor management.

Staying Too Connected

Susan is a sales rep at a company with a "no personal Internet use" policy. Susan has Net access, but she's supposed to use it only to review continually-updated loan rates, and to receive and reply to company emails.

Susan has a lot of friends and family, though; and staying in touch with them via her personal email, her Facebook account, and her Twitter account is too much of a temptation for her to resist. Susan therefore logs into each of these accounts several times a day. She reasons that it makes her a better employee, because feeling connected with loved ones while at work raises her morale and makes her more efficient. And anyway, she tells herself, it does no harm because no one at her office will ever know.

This works out fine for two years. Then one day Susan's manager calls her into his office. "Susan," he says, "a month ago the company installed 'spy' software that allows us to monitor what happens on every employee's computer. It found that you're spending about an hour a day on sites that have nothing to do with your job."

Susan turns red and starts to protest. Her manager motions to let him finish. "The company takes time theft as seriously as any other kind of theft. I'm afraid that I have to fire you, effective immediately."

Susan forcefully shakes her head. "I can't believe you spied on me!" she shouts. "That's a much bigger crime than my checking on how my family is doing! Not only am I not going to let you get away with firing me, I'm going to sue you for invasion of privacy!!"

Will Susan win her case?

Answer to *Staying Too Connected:*

Susan has no case.

Susan was using her company's computer on her company's time. The company is entitled to view and record every keystroke and mouse stroke Susan makes, just as it's entitled to watch her every move at her desk.

In addition, because Susan regularly violated her firm's clear rules about personal Internet use, her company will be able to successfully challenge her claim for unemployment benefits.

For her next job, Susan buys a handheld device that lets her cruise the Web during coffee breaks and lunch hours. This allows her to stay in touch with her family and friends without the risk of being spied on, and without stealing any time from work.

Fired for Pregnancy

Samantha is a single mom who works as a Holter technician—that is, she drives to visit a patient, applies heart monitors to the patient's chest, and then drives back a few days later to remove the monitors and analyze the readings. Samantha really enjoys doing this, and her performance record is flawless.

After several years on the job, Samantha misses two periods in a row, so she takes a pregnancy test. It's positive.

Samantha is ecstatic, but nervous about how her boss Boris will react. She remembers how he's complained about employees who have to leave early to pick up their children. She fears he'll be even more apprehensive about her situation because she doesn't have a husband as backup.

Samantha hides the news from Boris for several months. When she starts to show, however, Samantha can't keep it a secret any longer and so informs him. Boris responds, "Sheesh. Can you really afford another baby?" Samantha is taken back by this utter lack of support, but just replies, "Yes, I'm sure I can."

When Samantha arrives at work the next day, she finds a note from Boris that says, "Until you take your maternity leave, I don't want you driving the company vehicle anymore. The tires are too bald, and I don't want you to risk getting into an accident." So even though Samantha loves driving out to patients, she's confined to performing analyses of heart readings in the office.

The next week, Boris walks over to Samantha with one of her reports in hand and says, "I just read this and your analysis is incorrect. I'm disappointed in your work and am writing you up." Samantha is shocked. Before she can say anything, Boris adds, "If you make another mistake, I'm going to have to let you go."

Samantha is convinced Boris is setting her up to be fired. Rather than just wait for the ax to fall, Samantha files a charge of gender discrimination with the Equal Employment Opportunity Commission (EEOC).

Twenty days later, Boris receives a notice from the EEOC about Samantha's complaint. He's furious. Boris rushes over to Samantha and tells her, "How dare you file against me?! I've been nothing but nice to you. You know what? You're fired!"

Samantha is enraged; but she just calmly packs up her belongings and leaves. She tells herself that she expected to be fired anyway, and that she'll get justice from the EEOC…especially after she files a new charge, this time asserting unfair retaliation.

Is Samantha right?

Answer to *Fired for Pregnancy:*

Samantha will prevail.

Discrimination cases are usually hard to prove. However, Boris' note stating that Samantha won't be allowed to do her job anymore because of her pregnancy is strong evidence.

Even more damning, though, is Boris firing Samantha in direct response to receiving the EEOC notice. Both Federal and state laws prohibit retaliation against a worker exercising her rights in filing a discrimination claim.

Therefore, even if Samantha doesn't win her first suit, she's certain to win her case for retaliation, as the illegal nature of Boris' firing Samantha couldn't be more clear-cut.

Goading "Grandpa"

For the past three decades, Myron's worked in the deli section of a large supermarket. Now 74, Myron's exceptionally knowledgeable about meats and cheeses. He loves kibitzing with his customers and singing old show tunes to the ladies, activities which have built him a loyal following in the neighborhood.

Myron's deli section brings in lots of business, but the rest of the supermarket isn't performing as well as it should. The owners therefore decide their store needs major changes to modernize it. They reorganize the store's layout, renovate the shelves, brighten the lighting, and pipe in contemporary music. In addition, they hire a bunch of new workers and managers—all of whom are relatively young.

Myron welcomes the changes, recognizing they're genuine improvements that make the store livelier and attract more customers. Some of the workers kid with Myron, referring to him as "grandpa." Myron really is a grandfather, so he doesn't protest. When Myron's new manager Chuck hears these comments, he often giggles and chimes in, "If you see Myron's teeth lying around, be sure to tell me." Myron feels that goes beyond friendly banter, but bites his tongue because he doesn't want to get in trouble with his new boss.

Unfortunately, things only get worse. Chuck, who's 29, is constantly on Myron's back. "Myron," he says, "stop talking to the customers so much and focus on your job." Myron ignores such comments, knowing his customers come by for the conversation as much as for the meats and cheeses.

Chuck starts assigning Myron new menial duties, such as taking out the trash and mopping up the floor when the deli section isn't busy. Myron politely asks Chuck if he can assign these tasks to one of the workers who have fewer responsibilities. Chuck refuses, saying, "Myron, what's the matter, don't you have the energy?" Myron says nothing and does what he's told.

One morning a regular customer, Mrs. Patterson, comes into the deli and says she'd like Muenster cheese, but only if it's fresh. Myron takes a small slice of the cheese and tastes it. "Yes, it's very fresh. Would you like a pound?" Chuck is out of earshot, but he sees Myron's actions and comes running over. "What are you eating, grandpa?" A startled Myron replies, "I'm just tasting the cheese, what do you want from me?" Chuck replies, "You've just violated store policy." Myron, past his breaking point, responds, "For goodness sakes, stop bothering me. I'm trying to take care of Mrs. Patterson."

Chuck gives Myron a look and says, "Finish up with her and then come to my office."

When Myron does so, Chuck tells him, "We all like you here, but rules are rules. You're not allowed to eat the food. I have no choice but to fire you." Myron is furious. "Are you kidding me? I was just doing my job!" Chuck responds, "I'm sorry, but from where I stood it looked like theft."

A week later Myron stops by for his final paycheck and finds his deli section is being run by a young man in his early 20s.

Can Myron do anything about this situation?

Answer to *Goading "Grandpa"*

Most definitely. Myron should sue the supermarket for age discrimination.

It's common for markets to have rules against employees eating their food. However, an exception is made for tasting for the sake of quality control. Chuck must have been well aware of this...which means the theft charge was just an excuse.

That Myron's co-workers calling him "grandpa" was not only allowed but encouraged by his manager, and that Chuck followed up with even more outrageous remarks, indicates an environment hostile to Myron due to his age. The fact Myron was replaced by someone almost 60 years younger is further evidence age was the real reason for Myron's dismissal...and such discrimination is illegal.

It is unfortunate Myron neglected to maintain a journal documenting his bad treatment while working for Chuck, as this would've strengthened his case. Plus Myron will have trouble getting any co-workers to testify about how he was treated, since they're still employed by the supermarket. However, Myron has the perfect witness in Mrs. Patterson, who has nothing to fear from the store, knows Myron was just tasting the cheese, and heard Chuck call him "grandpa."

After Myron wins his lawsuit, he uses the money to retire and hang out with the beloved friends he's made in the neighborhood...and to eat cheese whenever he feels like it.

Dealing with Pests

Lori has been working five years for We Nab It, a pest control company. She visits dozens of clients each month to spray for unwanted bugs and rodents.

Lori is up for a promotion. To her surprise, her boss' boss Harry, who's at the top level of the company, decides to ride along one day and watch her operate.

Lori's first stop is a small duplex, where she demonstrates impressive speed and efficiency. Lori even shows Harry a more economical way in spraying, which if used by all the workers could save the company thousands of dollars each month.

Harry responds, "Lori, I knew you looked good in your outfit, but I had no idea you were this good at your job." Lori thinks Harry's comment is a little strange, but she lets it slide and keeps doing her best to service her clients effectively and economically.

After Lori services three more duplexes, Harry suggests they have lunch at a local diner. Lori agrees. The conversation over burgers and fries is casual but professional.

When they finish eating, Harry tells Lori he has to stop by his house to pick up some important documents for the office. When they arrive at his home, Harry invites Lori inside. Lori becomes a little suspicious of Harry's intentions and says, "Thank you, but I don't think that's necessary. I'll wait here in the truck."

Harry replies, "Don't be silly. It's hot in the truck. Come on in, it may take me a few minutes to gather these papers." Lori maintains her position, saying "No, it's fine. I can put the windows down to stay cool. And I have some paperwork to do."

"The documents I have inside are your promotion papers," says Harry. "I wanted you to take a look at them before I finalize them with the CEO." Harry then gently puts his hand on Lori's knee. "You know, your promotion will go a lot smoother if you come in and have a look at these papers."

Lori responds, "Excuse me." She takes Harry's hand off her knee and says, "Don't do that again."

Harry says nothing. He just gets out of the truck and goes into his house.

Lori is nervous and begins to shake. She can't believe what just happened. Instead of waiting for Harry to return, Lori speeds off in her truck and drives to the office.

When Lori arrives, she goes straight to the HR department to file a complaint against Harry.

The HR manager, Ms. Jones, sees Lori is upset and asks her to calm down. Ms. Jones pulls out a pad of paper and says, "Tell me what happened, Lori." Lori proceeds to describe the day's events. For the next 45 minutes, Ms. Jones listens intently, takes lots of notes, and appears genuinely concerned. As their conversation wraps up, Ms. .Jones assures Lori she'll investigate her allegations thoroughly.

Then Ms. Jones adds, "Let me ask you something. Do you think you might have misinterpreted Harry's actions?" Lori is stunned by the question. She firmly replies, "*No!* I can't believe you'd even suggest that." Lori shakes her head, leaves the office and goes home.

Did Lori do the right thing?

Answer to *Dealing with Pests:*

Lori had the right idea in reporting her boss, but she went about it the wrong way.

Lori should first contact the police and file a sexual harassment complaint against Harry. The police report will provide an official record of the date and time of the incident, and show that Lori took the matter seriously and acted promptly. It will also provide an objective record from the officer who takes Lori's statement. This could positively influence a judge or jury if a lawsuit is necessary.

In addition, Lori must immediately file a Charge of Discrimination/Sexual Harassment with the Equal Employment Opportunity Commission (EEOC). This will make it illegal for her company to fire her for complaining about what happened. The glare of the EEOC spotlight may also spur her company to go forward with Lori's promotion. Then again, if Lori's company is uncooperative, Lori's complaint lays the foundation for a lawsuit.

Lori should next see a psychologist to record the emotional effects Harry's actions have had on her. If Lori ends up having to sue the company, this will establish a basis for Lori collecting damages for mental anguish.

Once these wheels are in motion, Lori can contact an attorney who specializes in sexual harassment. Doing things in this order means no one can later claim an attorney put Lori up to filing her complaint.

These four steps—reaching out to the police, the EEOC, a psychologist, and an attorney—establishes the ideal foundation for Lori to succeed in a sexual harassment lawsuit.

As for HR, it exists to protect the company, not Lori. Everything Lori told Ms. Jones could be recorded in a way that appears most favorable to Harry; and Ms. Jones' report could then be used against Lori in court if Lori ends up suing.

That doesn't mean Lori shouldn't contact HR about what happened. She should, because it gives the company an opportunity to correct the situation. However, HR should be the last place Lori contacts, not the first. And before her HR interview, Lori should speak with her sexual harassment attorney to get advice on what to say and not say, which is likely to greatly reduce the opportunity for Lori's company to later use her words against her.

Short Skirts vs. Short Temper

Susan is a saleswoman at a jewelry store with five other employees and the owner, who's named Harry. Susan has an excellent sales record, so she's quite offended when one day Harry off-handedly remarks, "You know, you really should use makeup."

"What do you mean?!" Susan demands. "I *am* wearing makeup. Do you want me to cake it on?"

"I want you to apply it more attractively," Harry responds. "And while you're at it, wear shorter skirts."

Susan considers Harry's requests ridiculous. She assumes he had one drink too many at lunch, and she promptly forgets about the conversation.

A few days later, though, Harry approaches Susan again. "I told you to wear sexy makeup and hot skirts."

Susan is now seriously annoyed. "Harry, my face is fine. And my skirt barely covers my butt as is. I feel your comments are inappropriate, and they make me uncomfortable. Please drop this."

"Look, Susan, you're out here representing my store," replies Harry. "Part of my job is setting the image we project. Don't make this into some kind of civil rights protest. Just do what I say."

"I won't," Susan states flatly. "And if you don't change your mind by the end of the day, I'll quit."

Harry just shakes his head and walks away.

The next morning, Susan doesn't show up for work. At noon Harry receives this email from her: "Harry, I've resigned my position due to your sexual harassment. I'll be reporting you and the store to the EEOC. I'll also be claiming unemployment benefits. If you want to wear super-short skirts to attract customers, knock yourself out.—Susan."

Harry emails her back, "So long, you nutcase. File whatever you want. You won't get a penny beyond your final paycheck."

Who's right, Susan or Harry?

Answer to *Short Skirts vs. Short Temper:*

Susan may have the moral high ground. But legally, Harry is right.

The sexual harassment rules Susan referred to from the U.S. Equal Employment Opportunity Commission (EEOC) apply to companies with 15 or more employees. Since Harry's store employs only six people, he's exempt from these Federal statutes.

As for getting unemployment benefits, Susan would have to provide evidence of a pattern of harassment that interfered with her work and/or with her getting a raise. Harry's mere two requests for Susan to adjust her image to accommodate his vision for his store doesn't rise to the level of harassment a judge would require before granting benefits to an employee who quit.

Susan was certainly entitled to resign. But instead of reflexively dismissing Harry the first time he made his request, and then lashing out with an ultimatum the second time, she might've done better to consider Harry's perspective and try to negotiate some sort of middle ground that would've satisfied both of them. Instead, Susan's out of a high-paying job, and Harry's lost one of his best salespeople, because neither of them was willing to compromise on an issue for which they both had valid points of view.

Not Handicapped Accessible

Angie suffers from a degenerative hip disorder that prevents her from moving around without a mobilized wheelchair. However, this disability in no way diminishes the fact that Angie's an attractive and personable woman who loves working with people, making her a superb receptionist.

When her office unexpectedly goes under, Angie applies for work at a nearby major hotel chain. She excels at all the written tests, and passes three verbal interviews with flying colors, making her the top candidate. When the national headquarters receives the request to hire her, though, it balks.

Feeling bad, the head of the local hotel calls Angie to give her the bad news. "We all adore you," he says. "But our only opening right now is at the front desk, and headquarters told us your wheelchair would require demolishing our current desk and constructing a lower one to put you at eye level with customers. That would be expensive; but beyond the cost, headquarters requires each of its reception desks to have a uniform look across all its hotels. It won't permit our deviating from that look by making adjustments to our reception area. I'm really sorry."

Angie is understandably upset, but keeps her composure. "I really appreciate your considering me," she says. "Let me think about this and get back to you."

Is there anything Angie can do to get this job?

Answer to *Not Handicapped Accessible:*

Having a disability doesn't automatically entitle an applicant to special treatment. If Angie wasn't qualified for the position, or if she couldn't perform its essential tasks without the help of extraordinary accommodations, the hotel could easily say no to her.

In this case, however, headquarters claiming that hiring Angie would require a reconstruction of its front desk that would violate its uniformity rules is nonsense. Instead of lowering the desk, the hotel could simply "raise the floor" by creating an inexpensive removable ramp Angie could use while on duty. The main office's inability to think of such a simple alternative indicates the "uniformity" it's worried about may have nothing to do with its desks.

Angie did the right thing by behaving politely over the phone, but that doesn't mean she should give up. Her next step should be to contact the U.S. Equal Employment Opportunity Commission (EEOC), explain what happened, and hope the EEOC will look into the situation. The EEOC may "suggest" to the hotel main office that it try to be more creative in finding a solution before any formal action is taken.

Other resources Angie can turn to are the Job Accommodation Network (AskJan.org) and the Americans with Disabilities Act National Network (adata.org).

Punched in the Gut

Mark's been the supervisor of a golf club for 11 years. Under his guidance, the club transformed from a mediocre establishment that was losing money to a world-class profit-maker. Mark's last raise was three years ago and he believes he's overdue, so he calls the Chairman of the Board and schedules a meeting for the next day to discuss it.

When Mark arrives, he's surprised to see not only the Chairman, but also three other members of the Board. He greets them all politely. Then before he gets another word out, the Chairman says the last thing Mark expects to hear: "We like you, and you've shown tremendous loyalty and devotion to our club. However, we've decided to go in a different direction with a new supervisor."

Mark is stunned.

The Chairman continues, "We would like to offer you a nice severance package, which will take effect in four weeks."

"You mean I'll be here only another four weeks?" asks Mark.

"Yes, and not a day more."

Mark feels like he's about to explode, but he speaks calmly. "This is quite a surprise," he says. "Frankly, I feel like I just got punched in the gut. I came here today to ask for a raise and find out that I've been fired."

The Board members chuckle at his mention of a raise, but otherwise don't respond.

Mark realizes these men are ungrateful jerks. Part of him wishes he could make them understand everything he's done for the club. And part of him wants to tell them what pond scum they are.

What should Mark do?

Answer to *Punched in the Gut:*

It's clear Mark's getting no love from the Board members, so any attempt to defend himself would do nothing but open up a hornet's nest of unpleasantness.

Similarly, Mark going ballistic and calling the Board members every name in the book would not only fail to get his job back, it would jeopardize the "nice severance package" they promised him.

Instead, Mark should keep his cool, behave with thorough professionalism, and ask about the details of his severance package. He should also request that whatever is promised be supplied to him in writing as soon as possible. This will help ensure the Board members live up to their word—and allow Mark to secretly have the document reviewed by a labor attorney. Among the things his lawyer should check for is language that in any way jeopardizes Mark's unemployment benefits, as they might end up being worth as much as his severance.

Mark should also discuss what's expected of him during his last month. If the Board members ask that he train his replacement, he can agree to that, but he doesn't have to do a stellar job of it under the circumstances. Since his employers didn't appreciate the special insights and skills Mark provided, he needn't feel obliged to give away personal trade secrets before exiting—especially since they may give him a competitive edge when seeking his next position.

"But What About the Promotion?"

Lester is an assistant manager at a rental car agency. He's in the office of his supervisor, Mr. Davis, for his six month review. When Lester was hired he was told he'd probably be promoted to manager after six months, so he's brimming with excitement.

Mr. Davis begins by complimenting Lester for learning the ins and outs of his job quickly, and for his talent at creating instant intimacy with customers. Lester smiles happily.

"However," says Mr. Davis, "your punctuality is another matter. You've been coming in late on a regular basis. Sometimes it's just five minutes, but other times you've been as much as an hour off."

Lester is stunned his supervisor is aware of this— Mr. Davis' shift begins later in the morning, so he isn't around to see when Lester arrives. "Wow, I didn't realize...this was a problem," says Lester. "Yeah, I don't come in on the dot. But I usually stay an hour past my official end time to help last-minute customers and finish up paperwork. So I'm almost always putting in more than eight hours a day."

"You make it sound like you're overachieving," replies Mr. Davis. "But as far as I can tell, you're getting pretty much the same amount of work done as anyone else—except they show up on time. Maybe if you worked more efficiently, you wouldn't need to stay late."

Lester is reeling. "I see. Got you. Anything else I should know?"

Mr. Davis raises his eyebrow. "Now that you mention it, you have an attitude problem. On several occasions you've resisted when we've needed you to work a Saturday shift. And you can be counted on to make a fuss when asked to check out a car."

This evaluation isn't going remotely like Lester expected. He feels like shouting at Mr. Davis, but tries to control himself. "Tell you the truth, I had no clue you felt this way. This is the first I've heard about these things."

"Maybe it's the first time you've really been listening," replies Mr. Davis.

Lester shakes his head. "So is there anything else you're unhappy about?"

"Actually," says Mr. Davis, "I wasn't going to bring this up on top of everything else; but since you ask, I'd like to see you do better on convincing drivers to buy insurance on the cars you lease. That's a significant source of revenue for us; and while you're excellent at getting drivers to step up to more expensive rentals, you underperform when it comes to squeezing out those extra insurance dollars."

Lester's face reddens. Fighting to restrain himself, he just says, "Uh huh."

"Well," Mr. Davis continues, "aside from these points, we all enjoy working with you. And I look forward to your making improvements in your problem areas. I think that covers it, unless there's anything you'd like to say."

"Frankly," responds Lester, "I've worked really hard since Day 1 because I was told to expect a promotion to manager after six months. So what about the promotion?"

Mr. Davis blanches. "With that attitude of yours, you should be grateful you still have a job. Now get back to work, and think long and hard about what we've discussed."

What should Lester have done differently?

Answer to *"But What About the Promotion?"*

First, Lester should've understood that there are never any guarantees when it comes to promotions. Such decisions are made on a case-by-case basis, and are keyed to perceived performance.

Lester should've also been more in tune with what his manager really thought of him. For example, believing Mr. Davis didn't know about his perpetual lateness was naive of Lester; and so was assuming that staying late made up for it.

During his review, Lester should've asked for clarification on how important it is that he arrives precisely on time every morning, and whether he's scoring any points for working after hours. He could then align his office habits to his supervisor's expectations.

Further, Lester should've reined in his disappointment instead of effectively asking, "So what else don't you like about me?" His supervisor didn't come into the meeting with any plans to bash or embarrass, but Lester's childish petulance led Mr. Davis to rattle off the full list of Lester's flaws.

Finally, it was utterly inappropriate to ask about a promotion at the end of the review. Given Mr. Davis' problems with Lester's work habits and attitude, it came off as a bitter dig rather than a legitimate question.

Each of the issues Mr. Davis mentioned is fixable with effort on Lester's part. If Lester does exactly what Mr. Davis suggested—think about each request for improvement, and work hard on those areas—his next review could result in the promotion he's so eager to get. And at that point he'd be genuinely ready to take on its responsibilities.

The Calculating Contractor

Lisa, a freelance worker, is nearing the end of her three-year W2 employment contract at a prestigious firm. Two months before the contract is due to expire, Lisa asks her manager Mitch whether it's going to be renewed. He replies, "This isn't a good time to talk about it."

A month goes by, and Lisa asks again. Mitch says, "I still don't know. It's not my decision." Meanwhile, Lisa gets an offer from another company to work on a project that begins in three months. The other firm is promising her the same rate, and the work is likely to take at least four years. With no commitment from Mitch, Lisa decides to tell the other firm "yes."

A few days before her contract is due to end, Mitch tells Lisa, "We aren't going to renew your contract. But we'd like you to keep working for us without a contract. You'll get the same hourly rate. We just need to be flexible about how long we'll keep using you."

Lisa would prefer to continue working until her new assignment begins, so she's tempted to agree to this offer and then tell Mitch "so long" after two months. But because Lisa's had a lot of experience in the job market, she chooses to turn Mitch down.

Why didn't Lisa agree to Mitch's offer?

Answer to *The Calculating Contractor:*

When Mitch's company allows Lisa's contract to expire, it'll have the same effect as firing her—i.e., Lisa will be eligible for unemployment benefits.

However, if Lisa works for Mitch beyond the contractual period and then leaves for a new job, that will be the same as quitting her old job. In this case, Lisa will *not* be eligible for unemployment.

If everything works out with Lisa's new firm, this won't matter. But if the new project ends up not happening, or if Lisa doesn't get along with her new manager, or if anything else unexpected goes wrong, Lisa might quickly lose her new job. In this case, Lisa will have to rely on Mitch's company to provide unemployment benefits until she can find a new assignment...but Mitch's company will be obliged to do so only if Lisa leaves when her contract expires.

Lisa is experienced enough to know new projects don't always work out, so she decides to skip two months of salary in exchange for the safety net of unemployment benefits...and a well-earned vacation.

No Deposit, No Return

For nearly a year, Lou loaded bottles for soft drink distributor FizzCo. You might think this is a job anyone could handle. However, not only does Lou get himself fired, FizzCo challenges his claim for unemployment benefits on the basis of "sloppiness."

While Lou isn't the sharpest tool in the shed, he does one thing right: He hires me to represent him at his unemployment benefits hearing. I demolish his employer's case, making it clear that while Lou might not have been FizzCo's best worker, his performance wasn't poor enough to justify a denial of benefits.

The loss means FizzCo is on the hook for Lou's unemployment payments—and also an increase in its unemployment tax rate. The company is understandably unhappy about this. It considers filing an appeal, but concludes that'd be a waste of money because the judge did everything right. So instead it does something sneaky.

A few days later Lou's wife Rosie calls me. "You'll never believe it," she says. "FizzCo offered Lou his job back."

My heart sinks, because I can guess how Lou responded. "He accepted, didn't he?"

"Well, of course," Rosie says. "He likes the job. And he was worried that he wouldn't be able to find work anywhere else."

I didn't argue with Rosie, but had a pretty good idea of what would happen next.

Sure enough, just two weeks later FizzCo fires Lou again—and again contests his claim for unemployment benefits.

What should Lou have done differently?

Answer to *No Deposit, No Return:*

It might seem Lou was forced to agree to the job offer, because when you're on unemployment you're normally required to accept a position comparable to your last job.

Since the offer came from the company that fired him, though, Lou had some latitude in setting the terms under which he'd return. For example, Lou should've demanded a higher salary, and a written contract guaranteeing at least two years of employment. If FizzCo accepted, Lou would've been in good shape. And if FizzCo said no, Lou would've been free to continue receiving his unemployment checks.

But Lou's agreeing to come back with no preconditions gave FizzCo all the advantages. Lou's return to the workforce took FizzCo off the hook for his unemployment payments. And it gave FizzCo the opportunity to fire him again—and contest his benefits again.

Joanna's Job Hunt

Joanna's bank is going through rough times, and eliminating her loan officer position is one of the ways it chooses to reduce costs. HR provides Joanna with sterling references, and she's optimistic about being hired elsewhere.

Unfortunately, other banks are experiencing the same hard times, and Joanna had no success for several months.

Finally, Joanna spots an ad online for what seems like the perfect job for her. It combines her banking experience with her social skills, and also gives her an opportunity to work internationally. Joanna spends several hours making sure her cover note is flawless, and also makes small adjustments to her resume so it's a perfect fit for the job specs. After triple-checking everything, Joanna clicks her email program's *Send* button, and crosses her fingers.

A day goes by with no response. And then another. And another.

Joanna is frustrated. She can't imagine anyone being a better match for the position than she is, so why isn't the company at least contacting her for an interview? Joanna doesn't want to seem pushy, so keeps waiting and hoping.

When two whole weeks go by with no response, though, Joanna feels she has nothing to lose. The job ad didn't say "No calls," so she decides to phone the company to make sure her resume has been received and is in front of the right people.

The ad didn't mention anyone's name, so Joanna doesn't know who's in charge of evaluating the candidates. She therefore visits the company's Web site and carefully searches through it.

After an hour, Joanna finds a Mr. Goldberg who holds the same position she's applied for, only in a different department. She calls the company's general number and has the operator connect her to him.

Mr. Goldberg turns out to be a golden contact. "I'm very impressed with your credentials," he says, "and also with how well you handle yourself over the phone. I'd be happy to be your advocate. Forward your job application to my email address, and give me a little time to find out what's what."

A few days later, Joanna receives a call from Mr. O'Hara, the manager of the job she wants. "The only reason you haven't heard from me," he says, "is that right after the ad ran a project came up on a super-tight deadline. We received 300 applications for the job and haven't had time to look at any of them. Things will be back to normal in a week, though, and I'll definitely get in touch with you then."

Were Joanna's actions appropriate?

Answer to *Joanna's Job Hunt:*

Joanna showed creativity, diligence, and persistence in her pursuit of this job. She also was sufficiently professional when speaking with company staffers to make a positive impression. By demonstrating enthusiasm for the job and standing out from the crowd in a positive way, Joanna guaranteed herself an interview…and she ended up getting hired, beating out several other well-qualified candidates.

As long as you avoid violating the protocols of your field, don't be afraid to be creative in expressing your interest in a job and demonstrating qualities that show why you should be hired. Establishing connections with the right people can count for as much or more than what's on your resume.

Too Quick to Quit

Dave works as a salesman at a Honda car dealership with two other salespeople. He's been there for five years and likes his job. One day on his way home, however, Dave walks past a Porsche showroom with a Help Wanted sign. On a whim, he decides to interview for it.

Dave learns that the Porsche dealership will pay him both a higher salary and higher commission than he's currently making. He jumps at the chance to better himself and accepts the new position.

Dave submits his resignation at Honda. The following day he starts working for Porsche.

Unfortunately, after only a few hours, Dave has a rude awakening. There are 12 salespeople at the Porsche dealership; the customers are assigned by rotation; and due to the higher prices of the Porches, just a few customers come in each day. Dave's only option for staying afloat will be making cold calls and praying some of them turn into sales.

"This isn't what I expected," Dave says, and quits.

Dave then drives over to his Honda dealership and asks for his job back. However, he's already been replaced.

Dave files for unemployment. But because he resigned, his request is denied.

How could Dave have handled things better?

Answer to *Too Quick to Quit:*

There's nothing wrong with Dave wanting to improve his life by taking a better job. But he should've asked more detailed questions at his Porsche interview so he fully understood what he'd be signing up for.

In addition, Dave should've planned for the possibility his move wouldn't work out. His five years at the Honda dealership meant Dave had accumulated vacation days, sick days and/or personal days. He could've used them to try out working for the Porsche dealership. When Dave discovered the latter wasn't a good fit, he could've simply returned to his position at Honda without anyone knowing about his failed try at a new job.

The Bad Reference

Cindy works as a secretary for a radiologist located 70 miles from her home. She took the job because she'd planned to move to a small house near the office, but the real estate deal fell through. Cindy therefore has to drive over an hour to and from work each day.

Cindy tolerates this situation for three years. When the price of gas goes through the roof, however, she decides to be proactive and ask her boss for help.

"Dr. Fishman," Cindy says, "my commute is really starting to eat into my income. Would you consider increasing my salary by $100 a month to offset my gas expenses?"

Dr. Fishman smiles at her paternally. "Cindy, I'm crazy about you, but times are hard. I just can't afford the increase."

Cindy is disappointed, but responds professionally. "I understand," she says. "Unfortunately, I can't keep doing this. I have to give you my two weeks notice."

Dr. Fishman nods. "That's okay. I appreciate your three years of loyal and excellent work. Do you think you can extend another week if I can't find a replacement right away?"

"Oh, no problem," says Cindy.

"Terrific," Dr. Fishman says. "And needless to say, feel free to use me as a reference."

Cindy smiles. "Great! I'm sure I will."

Dr. Fishman does end up asking Cindy to stay the additional week, during which time she thoroughly trains her replacement.

After her last day, Cindy submits her resume to five potential medical employers, and then goes away for a week's well-earned vacation with no cell phone to distract her.

Shortly after Cindy leaves, Dr. Fishman can't find an important set of x-rays. He calls Cindy's home phone and cell, but reaches only her voice mail. He becomes furious, leaving stern messages. He eventually finds the x-rays, which aren't where they're supposed to be.

When Cindy returns from vacation, her mailbox holds letters of rejection from three of the offices to which she'd applied. They all use boilerplate language, telling her nothing about the reason for their decisions.

Cindy also hears Dr. Fishman's angry messages. The latter don't alarm her, though, because she's used to his flying off the handle when frustrated.

Cindy calls Dr. Fishman back immediately. "Are you missing me?" she asks playfully. Dr. Fishman pauses, and then says, "Oh yeah, you're one in a million."

"Did you find the missing x-rays?" Cindy asks.

Dr. Fishman takes a deep breath and replies, "Yes."

"Oh good," says Cindy. "By the way, did you receive any calls from employers inquiring about me?"

"No," responds Dr. Fishman, "none come to mind."

"Okay," says Cindy. "Please let me know if anyone gets in touch."

After the conversation ends, Cindy decides to follow up on the two employers who haven't yet responded. She calls one of them and gets the woman in charge of hiring. "Hello," says Cindy. "I was wondering if you received my job application."

"We did," replies the office manager, "but you weren't provided with a good reference by your previous employer."

"You must be mistaking me for someone else," says Cindy. "After all I've done for Dr. Fishman, I'm sure he has nothing but praise for me."

"I'm sorry, but it *was* Dr. Fishman. He said that you're disorganized, and that you misplace important x-rays, so he can't recommend you."

Cindy is stunned. "I see," she says. "Thank you for your honesty."

Cindy calls the other offices to which she applied. After some prompting, they all tell her the same story: "We're sorry, but Dr. Fishman gave you a bad reference."

What should Cindy have done differently?

Answer to *The Bad Reference:*

First, Cindy should've picked up on hints that Dr. Fishman is a bad employer and unconscionable liar.

If he'd been a good boss, Cindy wouldn't have needed to quit in the first place, because her request for an extra $25 a week for gas was a very reasonable one. His being too cheap to hang onto a loyal and hard-working employee, and manipulative enough to flatter Cindy so she'd give her all to training her less expensive replacement, should've raised alarm bells.

However, it wasn't until Dr. Fishman went out of his way to bad-mouth Cindy to all prospective employers that she realized what a small-minded narcissist he was.

Cindy should've been less trusting and more strategic. For example, she could've protected herself by asking Dr. Fishman for a letter of reference while still working for him. Her excuse could've been that she needed it to buy a new car, or even to be considered for purchasing a home closer to the office.

At minimum, Cindy should've asked for such a letter when she resigned and Dr. Fishman still needed her to train a replacement. With such a document in Cindy's possession, Dr. Fishman would've been more reluctant to say bad things about her; and if he did so regardless, Cindy would've been able to prove to prospective employers that he's two-faced and so lacks credibility. As is, all Cindy can do is explain the situation and hope that someone's willing to take a chance on her.

By the way, Cindy was lucky that her prospective employers were willing to be so frank about why they turned her down. It's common for many firms to reveal nothing. If you ever experience this, you may need to use a service such as Document Reference Check (badreferences.com) or Global Verification Services (global-verification.com) that will call your former employer, pretend to be interested in hiring you, and record your employer's comments about you. Knowing what's being said about you behind your back can empower you to counter any negative messages and reshape how the world perceives you.

ABOUT THE AUTHOR

Spencer Cohn began his career working for a law firm, focusing on probate law. His attention quickly turned one day as he learned of a single mother of four who'd been fired after notifying her employer she again, was pregnant. The mother was in desperate need of help for an upcoming unemployment hearing, however Mr. Cohn's employer refused to take her case because it wasn't sufficiently lucrative. Spencer volunteered to take her case—and won.

This experience was an eye-opener for Spencer who saw that he could actually make a significant difference in the lives of thousands of employees who have no expertise dealing with workplace issues.

Since 1989, he has devoted himself to unemployment law, representing more than 18,000 individual workers in a career spanning more than twenty years (and counting!).

Mr. Cohn's clients include every profession: executives, secretaries, doctors, nurses, policemen, teachers, software programmers, sanitation workers, security guards, accountants, athletes, and even an alligator wrestler! Also of note, Mr. Cohn won the decision for the Fed-Ex employee who was caught throwing boxes on delivery, gaining national attention from a video posted on YouTube.

Mr. Cohn's practice is based in South Florida, but currently has expanded nationwide. He has appeared as an unemployment law expert on national media outlets including NBC's "The Tonight Show with Jay Leno," CNN, FOX News, Sirius Satellite Radio, contributing to the Miami Herald and Credit.com, and has also been nominated as person 'Making a Difference' on "NBC News with Brian Williams".

Contact information

If you have your own workplace issue, you may contact Mr. Cohn toll free at (866) 805-9492 or email spencer@beattheboss.tv or through his website www.beattheboss.tv.

CPSIA information can be obtained
at www.ICGtesting.com
Printed in the USA
FSHW021429140919
61941FS